AMERICAN CIVIL LIBERTIES UNION

ACLU

HANDBOOKS FOR YOUNG AMERICANS

The Rights of Students

EVE CARY

ALAN H. LEVINE

JANET PRICE

PUFFIN BOOKS

To Norman Dorsen,
with thanks

And to Richard,
with love
—E. C.

PUFFIN BOOKS
Published by the Penguin Group
Penguin Putnam Inc., 375 Hudson Street, New York, New York 10014, U.S.A.
Penguin Books Ltd, 27 Wrights Lane, London W8 5TZ, England
Penguin Books Australia Ltd, Ringwood, Victoria, Australia
Penguin Books Canada Ltd, 10 Alcorn Avenue, Toronto, Ontario, Canada M4V 3B2
Penguin Books (N.Z.) Ltd, 182-190 Wairau Road, Auckland 10, New Zealand

Penguin Books Ltd, Registered Offices: Harmondsworth, Middlesex, England

First published in the United States of America by Puffin Books,
a member of Penguin Putnam Inc., 1997

1 3 5 7 9 10 8 6 4 2

LIBRARY OF CONGRESS CATALOGING-IN-PUBLICATION DATA
Cary, Eve.
The rights of students / Eve Cary, Alan H. Levine, Janet Price ;
foreword by Norman Dorsen.
p.   cm.—(ACLU handbooks for young Americans)
Price's name appears first on the previous edition.
Summary: Explains the legal rights and obligations that pertain to students,
including such topics as free education, freedom of expression, personal
appearance, corporal punishment, grades, school records, and more.
Includes bibliographical references and index.
ISBN 0-14-037784-0 (pbk.)
1. Students—Legal status, laws, etc.—United States—Juvenile literature.
[1. Students—Legal status, laws, etc.]   I. Levine, Alan H.   II. Price, Janet, R.
III. Title.   IV. Series: ACLU handbook for young Americans.
KF4150.C29   1997   344.73'079—dc21   97-18976   CIP   AC

Printed in U.S.A.
Set in ITC Century Book

CONTENTS

FOREWORD

This guide sets forth the rights of students under the present law and offers suggestions on how they can be protected. It is one of a series of handbooks for young adults which is published in cooperation with the American Civil Liberties Union (ACLU).

This guide offers no assurances that the rights it discusses will be respected. The laws may change, and in some of the topics covered in these pages they change quite rapidly. An effort has been made to note those parts of the law where movement is taking place, but it is not always possible to predict accurately when the law *will* change.

Even if the laws remain the same, their interpretations by courts and administrative officials often vary. In a federal system such as ours, there is a built-in problem since state and federal law differ, not to mention the confusion between states. In addition, there are wide variations in how particular courts and administrative officials will interpret the same law at any given moment.

If you encounter what you consider to be a specific abuse of your rights, you should seek legal assistance. There are a number of agencies that may help you, among them ACLU affiliate offices, but bear in mind that the ACLU is a limited-purpose organization. In many communities, there are federally funded legal service offices which provide asistance to persons who cannot afford the costs of legal representation. In general, the rights that the ACLU defends are freedom of inquiry and expression, due process of law, equal protection of the laws, and privacy. The authors in this series discuss other rights (even though they sometimes fall outside the ACLU's usual concern) in order to provide as much guidance as possible.

These publications carry the hope that Americans, informed of their rights, will be encouraged to exercise them. Through their exercise, rights are given life. If they are rarely used, they may be forgotten and violations may become routine.

It is of special importance that young people learn what their rights are and that there is such a thing as "rights"—individual liberties that the government, no matter how strong, must honor. Only a self-confident country can remain faithful to such a vision, and young people are the future of all countries, whether or not these recognize the value of rights to a thriving civilization. The handbooks in this series are designed to contribute to this goal.

Norman Dorsen
Stokes Professor,
New York University School of Law
President, ACLU 1976–1991

ACKNOWLEDGMENTS

This book is an updated and substantially rewritten version of *The Rights of Students* by Alan H. Levine, Eve Cary, and Janet Price, which was part of the continuing series of handbooks published in cooperation with the American Civil Liberties Union. Much of the material in the original book was drawn from the experience of the New York Civil Liberties Union's Student Rights Project directed by Alan Levine for two years during the 1970s, which helped students in New York City's public schools secure the rights discussed in this book. Also instrumental in securing these rights was Advocates for Children of New York, Inc., an organization that works in a variety of ways to make the public schools more responsive to the needs of students and their parents.

Several people helped in the preparation of this book. Thanks are due in particular to Elizabeth Antoine for her patient and cheerful typing and retyping of the manuscript, and to Brooklyn Law School students David O'Connor, Michael Smith, Dawn Furlong, Robert Cronk, and Gisèle Heldt for their excellent research assistance.

1

INTRODUCTION

In order to understand what your rights are as a public-school student, you need to understand something about how our legal system works. As you know, the basic document that sets up our legal system is the United States Constitution. The Constitution explains how we elect the government of the United States, and it gives the government the specific powers it needs in order to run the country. These include the power to pass laws that are "necessary and proper" for carrying out the other powers. The government does not have the power to do anything that the Constitution does not permit it to do. Therefore, when you are thinking about your rights, a better question to ask than, "Do I have the right to do this?" is "Does the government have the right to stop me from doing this?"

Although the government may not forbid you to do something unless the Constitution says it can, the people who wrote the Constitution thought that certain rights are so important that they should be specifically guaranteed. Therefore, the writers added ten amendments to the Constitution which together are known as the Bill of Rights. (An amendment is an addition or alteration to a constitution or law.) The Bill of Rights lists the most important rights that the government may never deny to its citizens.

Four of the amendments that make up the Bill of Rights are particularly important for students.

The First Amendment says two important things. First:

> *Congress shall make no law . . . abridging the freedom of speech, or of the press; or the right of the people peaceably to assemble, and to petition the government for a redress of grievances.*

This means that you cannot be forbidden from or punished for expressing your opinions out loud or in print, either on your own or with a group of other people.

The second thing the First Amendment says is that

> *Congress shall make no law respecting an establishment of religion, or prohibiting the free exercise thereof.*

This means that the government can neither prohibit you from practicing your religion nor can it encourage you to practice any religion. In short, religion is none of the government's business.

The Fourth Amendment says:

> *The right of the people to be secure in their persons, houses, papers, and effects, against unreasonable searches and seizures, shall not be violated, and no Warrants shall issue, but upon probable cause, supported by oath or affirmation, and particularly describing the place to be searched, and the persons or things to be seized.*

This means that the police may not search you or your property, nor can they arrest you, unless they have a very good reason for believing that you have committed a crime. Moreover, they cannot search your house or other private place belonging to you without a warrant signed by a judge who has decided that there is a very good reason to believe that you have committed a crime.

The Fifth Amendment says:

No person shall . . . be deprived of life, liberty, or property without due process of law.

This means that the government may not punish you without giving you a fair chance to defend yourself.

Finally, the Fourteenth Amendment says:

No State shall deprive any person of life, liberty or property without due process of law; nor deny to any person within its jurisdiction the equal protection of the laws.

This amendment means that, just as the federal government may not punish you without giving you a fair chance to defend yourself, the government of a state cannot do so either. Moreover, all laws must apply equally to all citizens who are, for legal purposes, the same as one another. For example, the government may not pass a law saying that people of one race are allowed to do something that people of another race are not allowed to do. (It may, however, pass laws that apply to children, but not to adults, since children are not always the same as adults. For example, laws requiring children, but not adults, to go to school are constitutional, as are laws prohibiting children from buying alcohol and cigarettes.)

Before going any further, it is important to understand two things. First, when "the government" is mentioned in this book, it means not only the people whom we have elected to represent us, such as the president and senators, but also the people who are hired to work for the government, such as police officers and public-school principals. All of these people must obey the Constitution when they are performing their jobs.

Second, the Constitution governs the conduct *only* of people who work for the government. It does not apply to private people. This means, for example, that while the principal of a public school cannot make students say prayers in class because that would violate the First Amendment guarantee of freedom of religion, the principal of a parochial (religious) or other private school can require students to pray. The rights of students in private schools under federal and state laws are discussed in chapter 12.

The United States Constitution is not the only source of rights. Each state has its own constitution. Many of the provisions of these state constitutions are the same as those in the United States Constitution, but they apply only to the actions of state officials. Thus, a public-school principal in New York is prohibited from holding religious services in school, not just by the federal Constitution, but also by the New York State Constitution.

Just because private individuals are not governed by either federal or state constitutions does not mean that there are no limitations on their actions. Both Congress and the legislatures of all of the states pass laws that apply to private people as well as to government officials. The laws enacted by Congress are for the whole country. Those passed by the state legislatures are just for the people of that state. So people in New York may have more or fewer or different rights and obligations than do people in Louisiana. For example, in Louisiana anyone over the age of eighteen can buy alcohol, while in other states the legal drinking age is twenty-one.

Just as we have separate federal and state governments, we also have separate systems of federal courts and state courts. The job of the federal courts is to interpret federal laws; the job of the state courts is to interpret state laws. Both types of courts have the power to interpret the United States Constitution. In addition, the state courts can interpret their own state constitutions.

In this book you will hear about lawsuits that students have brought in either federal or state courts. In these lawsuits, the students have asked the courts to declare that certain actions by school officials are unconstitutional. In the federal court system, there are three levels of courts. The district courts are the trial courts that hear evidence and then reach a decision. If a party to a lawsuit does not like a decision of the district court, that person can then appeal to one of the thirteen United States Circuit Courts of Appeal, which hear appeals from several different districts. If a party does not like the decision of the Circuit Court of Appeals, that person can then ask the Supreme Court of the United States to decide the case. There are too many cases for the Supreme Court to decide all of them. Instead, the Court agrees to decide only the most important cases.

Each state also has its own court system. All are a little different, but each works basically the same way the federal court system works, with a trial court at the bottom that hears evidence, and then two levels of appellate courts. Below is a diagram of the federal court system and of three typical state court systems.

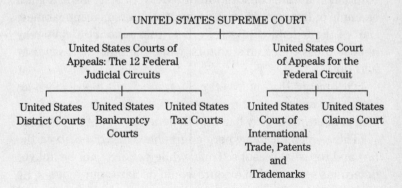

UNITED STATES SUPREME COURT

United States Courts of Appeals: The 12 Federal Judicial Circuits

United States Court of Appeals for the Federal Circuit

United States District Courts

United States Bankruptcy Courts

United States Tax Courts

United States Court of International Trade, Patents and Trademarks

United States Claims Court

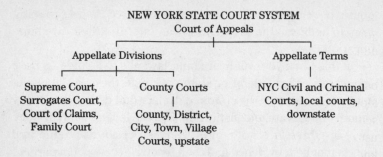

NEW YORK STATE COURT SYSTEM
Court of Appeals

Appellate Divisions — Appellate Terms

Supreme Court, Surrogates Court, Court of Claims, Family Court — County Courts / County, District, City, Town, Village Courts, upstate

NYC Civil and Criminal Courts, local courts, downstate

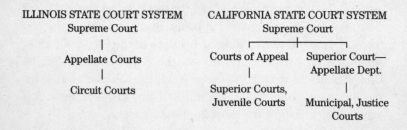

ILLINOIS STATE COURT SYSTEM
Supreme Court
Appellate Courts
Circuit Courts

CALIFORNIA STATE COURT SYSTEM
Supreme Court

Courts of Appeal — Superior Court—Appellate Dept.

Superior Courts, Juvenile Courts — Municipal, Justice Courts

As you will see as you read this book, the many different courts do not always agree with each other about whether particular actions by state officials violate either the federal Constitution or a state constitution or federal or state laws. A good example of this is in the area of students' personal appearance. Half of the federal courts have held that school officials may impose dress codes on students, while the other half say they may not.

This means that, unless the Supreme Court has decided an issue, the answer to the question "Can the principal of my school make me cut my hair?" is "It depends on where you live."

This book indicates where courts have disagreed about the law and for what reasons. Thus, while you may not be able to determine exactly what a court would declare your rights to be in a particular situation, you will learn some of the arguments you can make to support your position in any dispute with the administrators of your school about your rights.

Finally, keep in mind that going to court has many drawbacks. Litigation is usually expensive and takes a very long time. Moreover, in most situations, courts are likely to agree with school officials, rather than with students. This is because judges usually believe that school officials are experts in education and know best how schools should be run. Therefore, your best bet in most situations is to try to come to an agreement with school officials about your rights and save litigation as a last resort.

2

THE RIGHT TO A FREE PUBLIC EDUCATION

Do children have to go to school?

Most kids have asked, at one time or another, "Do I *have* to go to school?" The answer to that question is, "Yes, you do, if you are between the ages of six and sixteen years old [state laws vary somewhat] and have not yet graduated from high school." If you think that the obligation to attend school for several hours every weekday during most months of the year is a big interference with your liberty, you are perfectly right. Indeed, the government can impose such a duty on you only for a very good reason. That reason, of course, is that we live in a complicated world and most jobs today require education. Our country needs its citizens to be well educated so that they can do their jobs and support themselves and participate in running the government. The need for a well-educated population is so important to our country that it justifies the laws that require kids to go to school.

Do children have the right to go to school?

Yes. Even more important than the fact that you have the *oblig-*

ation to attend school is the fact that you have the *right* to do so—free of charge. Indeed, although you are allowed to leave school when you are sixteen, whether or not you have graduated, you have the right to continue your education until you are twenty-one or you graduate from high school, whichever comes first. Since most people's chances of getting a good job and earning a good living depend on their obtaining at least a high-school diploma, your right to a free public education is one of the most valuable rights you have. Because it is so important, it cannot be taken away from you as a punishment for bad behavior except in rare circumstances—and then only with strict safeguards to make sure that such a severe punishment is necessary. Therefore, if a school official tries to expel or even suspend you from school, get legal help right away. This is discussed in chapter 6.

Do children have the right to attend a public school of their choice?

No. Your right to a free public education does not necessarily mean that you may attend any school you choose. Laws that require students to attend the school in the community in which they live are valid. School districts can even require that you attend school where your parents or legal guardian live, even though you might prefer living with a friend or relative located in a better school district so that you can attend school there. Only a student who is "emancipated"—which means that he or she is not supported financially by a parent and has set up an independent household—does not have to attend school in a parent's district but can go to the school in the district where he or she is actually living. If school officials do not believe that the place where you are living is your legal residence and therefore believe you do not have the right to attend a school in that district, you must be given the chance to prove

9

that it is your legal residence and, in most places, to continue attending the school of your choice while the issue is being resolved.

Do children have the right to attend a public school near home?

No. The right to a free public education also does not guarantee you the right to attend a school that is near your home. For example, in some small, remote communities in Alaska, there are no schools. The highest court in Alaska has held that the state did not have to establish schools in these places as long as it arranged for students to live away from home and attend school in another community.

Can students be required to pay for their books in school?

Sometimes. One problem for many students is that although they are allowed to attend public school for free, once they get to school they are asked to pay for books or other materials that are used in school. Some courts have ruled, however, that charging fees for educational materials violates the right to a free public education. For example, in 1970 some students in Idaho went to court to challenge a school rule that required students to pay a $25.00 fee each year for textbooks and extra-curricular activities. Students who did not pay the fee would not receive their official transcripts from the school. The students argued that the fee requirement violated their right to a free education. The school responded by saying that withholding the transcripts did not deny students an education—they had already received that.

But the court agreed with the students. It ruled that the right to a free education guarantees more than just the right to attend school. It also guarantees the right to receive every "necessary element" of an education—for example, a transcript—for free. Therefore, the Idaho court ruled, schools in that state may never charge fees for textbooks. Courts in North Dakota and Wisconsin have held that schools must also provide any other equipment that is necessary for students to participate in regular classes. A court in Missouri ruled that schools cannot make students pay to register for regular academic courses.

Other state courts have held, however, that fees are permissible in public schools, at least in some circumstances. For example, a New Mexico court held that a school could charge students fees to register for nonrequired courses. Under Illinois law, textbooks must be provided for free, but schools may charge for other educational materials such as workbooks, maps, and laboratory supplies. Courts in several states have held that schools may charge rental fees for textbooks. In almost all of them, however, it is the law that when rental fees are charged, the school must still provide free books and necessary materials to students who cannot afford them.

Can students be required to pay to participate in extracurricular activities?

There is a lot of disagreement among courts about whether schools can charge students to participate in extracurricular activities. The highest court in California, for example, found that both the state constitution and state regulations prohibited schools from charging for extracurricular activities because such activities were an important part of a public-school student's education. On the other hand, a Michigan court reached the opposite conclusion in a lawsuit filed against two school districts that made students pay to participate in athletics. The court held that although the schools could not charge students for academic materials, athletics were "extra" and therefore

11

the school was not required to provide them at no cost to students. The court also found that the charge was permissible because the school did not require students to pay the fee if they could not afford to do so.

As you can see, the law differs from place to place concerning exactly what rights are encompassed by the right to a free public education. However, these cases suggest that the first question you should ask if your school charges you a fee for materials or activities is whether the material or activity is a necessary part of your education. The more necessary it is, the stronger your argument is that it should be provided free of charge. The second question you should ask, if you cannot afford to pay the fee, is whether there is a school regulation that allows students in your situation to receive the material or participate in the activity free of charge. Although the Supreme Court of the United States has never decided the issue, it is likely that it would hold that it is unconstitutional for a school to refuse to provide necessary books and equipment to students who cannot pay for them. In any case, most schools already have a confidential procedure for students to request that they not be required to pay a fee if it would be hard for them to do so. Don't be embarrassed to demand your right to a free education.

3

EQUAL PROTECTION

Do *all* children in the United States have the right to go to school?

Yes. The right to attend school belongs equally to all children who live in the United States, no matter what their race or sex or religion or ethnic background, whether they are American citizens or illegal residents who speak no English, whether they are married or have children, or whether they suffer from a physical or mental disability. While you have the right not to be discriminated against in school for any of these reasons, the law is somewhat different depending on the basis for the discrimination. For example, boys and girls can sometimes be treated differently, as can students with disabilities.

Can schools ever discriminate against students on the basis of race?

No, never. One of the most important cases the Supreme Court ever decided, *Brown v. Board of Education,*[1] established that state law requiring separate schools for children of different races violated the constitutional guarantee of equal protection. That case was decided in 1954. Since that time, hundreds of cases have been brought in which students have argued that different school policies have discriminated against them because of their race. These cases involve many different situations. The important thing to remember is that you have an absolute right to be free of race discrimination in school. If you believe you are being discriminated against, you should go to a lawyer or to an organization in your community that deals with such complaints. The same is true if you are discriminated against because of your religion or the country you or your family comes from.

Can schools ever discriminate against students on the basis of sex?

No. The Constitution and various federal and state laws also prohibit schools from discriminating against students on the basis of their sex. Sex discrimination is a bit more complicated than race discrimination, because while there is never a good reason for treating people of different races differently, occasionally (although rarely) there may be a good reason for treating boys and girls differently. The question in each case is whether there really is a very good reason for the different treatment.

Are all-boys or all-girls schools legal?

Probably not. Although *Brown v. Board of Education* made it clear that separate schools for children of different races can never be equal and are therefore unconstitutional, it is not completely decided whether it is also unconstitutional for a public-school district to have separate schools for boys and for girls. It is well established that if a school distict offers in one school a special program that is not offered at any other school, it would be illegal to exclude students of either sex from the special school. A Pennsylvania court in 1977, however, allowed a school district to maintain two separate schools for academically gifted students, one for boys and one for girls. But the Supreme Court has said that before a court will permit a school district to have single-sex schools, it must have an "exceedingly persuasive justification" (that is, a very, very good reason) for it. There are not many such justifications that courts are likely to find extremely persuasive. A more recent Supreme Court decision striking down the exclusion of women from a military college in Virginia indicates, however, that separate-sex public elementary and high schools may not be constitutional. Therefore, if you are excluded from a public school that you would like to attend because of your sex, you should ask a lawyer to find out if the discrimination is legal.

Can a public school have fixed quotas for girls and boys?

No. Federal law prohibits sex quotas. That is, schools may not decide to admit only fixed numbers of boys or girls. Sometimes specialized public schools that require an entrance examination have set a fixed number of places for boys and girls, and thus measure boys' scores against those of other boys and girls' scores against those of girls. This meant in one Boston school that some boys were admitted who had lower scores than those of girls who were rejected. The girls brought a lawsuit challenging this practice and in 1975 the court agreed with them. It said that sex quotas are unfair and that in the future, all applicants had to be measured against each other, even if that meant that the class would consist of unequal numbers of boys and girls. A California court reached the same conclusion in a similar case in 1975.

15

Can a public school limit particular classes to students of one sex?

No. Once you are in school, you also have the right not to be discriminated against on the basis of sex. This means that there cannot be separate courses for boys, such as shop or automechanics, from which girls are excluded, and others for girls, such as home economics, from which boys are excluded.

Can a public school have single-sex athletic teams?

This question is a bit complicated. While in most situations boys and girls are the same (for example, boys can learn to cook as well as girls, and girls can learn to repair cars as well as boys), there are real physical differences between boys and girls that in many (but not all) situations may prevent them from competing equally in athletic events.

Both the Constitution and federal law require that boys and girls be provided with equal athletic opportunities. Different courts have interpreted this requirement to mean different things. Many courts have held that boys and girls may always be separated in contact sports. They have also held that separate teams for boys and girls are permissible in all sports, as long as the school provides students of both sexes with the opportunity to participate in the particular sport. This means that in some states, a school would be allowed to have a boys' football team, but no football team for girls, since football is a contact sport. The school would also be permitted to have separate teams for boys and girls in non-contact sports, such as tennis.

But in other states, courts have held that girls have the right to participate on boys' teams if they are capable of doing so, even where there is a separate team for girls, and even in contact sports. These courts said that just because *most* girls might not be able to compete with boys, this is no reason for excluding the unusual girl who *can* compete. In these states, students of both sexes must be able to try out for the same teams. If it turns out that the best players are all boys, an all-boy team is permitted. In this situation, however, the girls who did not make the team must be permitted to try out for an all-girl team.

The rule is a bit different for boys who want to participate on girls' teams. In this situation, boys can be excluded from an all-girl team, even where there is no boys' team in the same sport, as long as the overall athletic opportunities for boys at the school are as good as or better than they are for girls. This difference in the law for boys and girls has been upheld by courts because, in the past, girls have been discriminated against in athletics and the goal of the law is to make up for that past discrimination. This law may very well change in the future, so if you are a boy and are being excluded from a girls' team, you might ask a lawyer to look into the situation for you.

Just remember that whatever the precise law is in your state, in all states girls and boys must be given equal, if not identical, opportunities to participate in school athletics. If you believe that your school is not treating boys and girls equally and that because of your sex you are being denied the right to participate in a sport you enjoy, it is worthwhile to consult a lawyer.

What can a student do about sexual abuse or harassment by a school employee or by another student?

Students have an absolute right not to be sexually abused or harassed by a school employee. If school officials are, or should have been, aware that a teacher or other school employee has sexually abused a student, the student can sue the school as well as press charges against the employee personally. The courts are divided on the question of whether a student may sue school officials under Title IX for failing to prevent another student from sexually harassing her or him and thus creating a sexually hostile learning environment. The federal court of appeals in Georgia held that students may not hold school officials responsible for the actions of other students, while the federal court of appeals in Texas held that they may. The Department of Education Office of Civil Rights, which is the office in charge of interpreting Title IX, agrees with the Georgia court. Therefore, if you are being sexually harassed by a fellow student, be sure to demand that school officials protect you. If they do not, you will have a strong argument that they are breaking the law.

Can schools refuse to admit students who are married or pregnant or who have children?

No. In the past, schools often prohibited students from attending school or participating in extracurricular activities when they got married or became pregnant or had children. Now, federal law prohibits schools from discriminating against married or pregnant students or students who have children. This is a good thing, since, in the words of a Kentucky court, there is "no reason to suppose that the marriage of a student would diminish the need of that student for an education—indeed, just the contrary would appear to be the case." The same thing is true, of course, for students who are, or will soon become, parents, whether or not they are married.

Can pregnant students be forced to attend special classes?

No. Many schools have separate programs for pregnant pupils. The decision whether to attend such a program or to stay in regular classes is up to the pregnant student, whether she is married or unmarried. She may not be excluded from regular classes if she wishes to attend them. Moreover, any special program must be educationally equal to the regular program.

Can married or pregnant students or students with children be prohibited from participating in extra-curricular activities?

No. Sometimes school officials try to prohibit married and pregnant students and students with children from participating in extracurricular activities. These rules violate the Constitution and federal law. This is important because, as many courts have said, participation in extracurricular activities is an important part of school and often influences a student's chances of getting into college.

There are several cases that uphold the right of married and pregnant students to participate in extracurricular activities. For example, in 1985 an unmarried, pregnant student in Illinois was dismissed from the National Honor Society because school officials believed that her pregnancy proved that she did not meet the society's standards for leadership and character. A court held, however, that her dismissal violated her right not to be discriminated against on the basis of sex.

Another court disagreed with this decision, however, and held that the dismissal of an unmarried pregnant student from the National Honor Society was unlawful. The court found that the student was not dismissed because she was pregnant but because she engaged in premarital sex. The court indicated that the rule against permarital sex had to apply equally to boys and girls or it would be illegal sex discrimination.

In another case, in Indiana, school officials refused to allow married students to participate in interscholastic sports. They said that married students should be earning a living for their families after school and not playing sports. The court held that this reason might be true for unmarried students, too, and that in any case, students who are mature enough to be married are mature enough to make their own decisions about how to provide for their families.

In some cases, school officials have argued in court that if married students are allowed to participate in sports and other extracurricular activities, they may talk about sex to their fellow students and cause disciplinary problems. The courts in the cases in which these arguments were made found no evidence that this was true, and ordered the schools to allow the students to participate in extracurricular activities. The New York Commissioner of Education in 1972 likewise found that school officials had not produced a good reason for prohibiting a married, pregnant student from attending her graduation and therefore ordered that she be allowed to do so since she had met all of the academic requirements to graduate.

The point to keep in mind in any dispute with school officials is that they must be able to show that any special rules for pregnant or married students are necessary for the school to run properly. If they cannot do this—and they rarely can—the rule discriminates unfairly.

Can schools refuse to admit children because they are not United States citizens?

No. All children who live in the United States have the right to attend public school, whether or not they are citizens.[2] Even children whose parents are in this country illegally have the right to a free public education. This means that if you come from another country, when you register to go to school, school officials may not make you show citizenship papers or green cards or any other document to prove that you are a citizen or that it is legal for you to live in the United States. There are also special laws that guarantee a free public education to the children of migrant workers who live in the United States for only part of the year. These laws guarantee that these children must be given the opportunity to make up work and to earn credit for attending school, even though they have had to miss parts of the school year because of their parents' jobs. Just remember, no matter where your parents have come from and no matter whether they are supposed to be in the United States or not, as long as you are here, you have the right to go to school.

Do schools have to provide instruction to students who do not speak English?

Yes. Your right to an education does not mean simply that you have the right to sit in a classroom for six hours and then go home. It means that you have the right to an education that is appropriate for you. Thus, students who do not speak English have the right to require school districts to provide them with either bilingual classes or English-language instruction, or both.

Schools may meet their legal obligation to provide non-English-speaking students with a good education with different types of programs. At a minimum, a school must identify all children who are not fluent in English. Then it must test them to determine how well they speak English and what academic level they have reached in their native language. Then it must provide an educational program that teaches the student to understand and speak in English well enough to move into regular classes. The school has a duty to provide teachers who are trained to teach non-English-speaking students and to make sure that the program in fact teaches children to speak English and to keep up in other subjects while they are learning the language.

The goal of any bilingual program is to teach children to speak English quickly and well enough so that they can join their English-speaking classmates. Therefore, just as you have the right to a bilingual program if you need one, you also have the right to leave such a program if you do not need one. You and your parents should talk to your school's administrators if you are not getting the program you need or want.

Do students with disabilities have the right to an education?

Yes. Two important federal laws guarantee students who have mental or physical disabilities the right to a free and appropriate public education.[3] In addition, each state has statutes and regulations that explain in detail exactly how a good education is to be provided to students with disabilities. Many states provide disabled students with even more services and rights than they are required to do by federal law.

Which children are considered "disabled"?

Under federal law, the term "children with disabilities" means children who are mentally retarded, hard of hearing or deaf, totally or partially blind, speech-impaired, orthopedically impaired (which means that they have trouble moving in some way), generally in poor health, or who have specific learning disabilities such as the inability to learn to read. In short, a person is defined as disabled under the law if he or she has a physical or mental problem that limits at least one of life's major activities.

What is considered an "appropriate education" for students with disabilities?

It depends on the student. The federal law has two purposes regarding this issue. The first purpose is to identify disabled students so that they can receive the special education they need in order to learn. For example, deaf students may be entitled to have sign-language interpreters, and students who are mentally retarded have the right to attend special classes where they can learn skills that will help them lead independent lives. The second purpose of the law is to provide procedures to make sure that students are not placed in special-education classes when they are *not* learning-disabled.

For example, you cannot be placed in a program for emotionally disturbed students just because school officials say that you do not get along well with other students. Similarily, you cannot be placed in a program for the mentally retarded because you do badly on a standard IQ test.

What is an "appropriate" education must be determined for each student, usually by experts such as teachers, doctors, or psychologists who have worked with a student and with the student's parents. The Supreme Court said in 1982 that an "appropriate" education does not necessarily mean the best education possible. Thus, a deaf student in New York who was able to do above-average work in school was not entitled to have the school provide her with a sign-language interpreter, which would have made it possible for her to do even better. In 1972 the Supreme Court held that the school only had to provide her with a program that was "reasonably calculated" to allow her to benefit from her education. Some states, however, have stronger laws that guarantee disabled children the right to an education that will allow them to "reach their full potential" or to "achieve educational success." Courts in these states have held that the schools must do more than provide disabled students with just some education. This means that if you are doing badly in school with a particular program, the school may be required to provide you with a better one.

Are students with disabilities required to attend special classes?

The right to an appropriate education does not just mean that schools must provide special programs and services for disabled students who need them. It also means that disabled students who do *not* need special programs must be permitted to attend regular classes. Schools may not place disabled students in special classes that they do not need simply because, for example, the school building has no elevators or narrow doors or bathrooms too small for a wheelchair. The law is clear that students with disabilities have the right to use the regular school building and it is the duty of the school to build ramps or hold classes on the first floor or do whatever else is necessary to make it possible for disabled students to join the rest of their classmates.

The Federal Department of Education's Office of Civil Rights held in 1980 that making arrangements for someone to carry a disabled student from place to place did not meet the school's duty to make the school accessible to all students. Another court held that a disabled student could not be made to attend a school in another district when it was possible to make the school in his own district accessible to him.

Whenever it is possible to do so, the statute requires that disabled students must be placed in the "least restrictive environment" possible. This means that whenever possible, they must be given help that will allow them to attend regular classes with extra services, rather than being placed in a special class just for disabled students. These services might include special equipment or materials that the student can use, an assistant for the teacher to help the student, or a few extra classes or tutoring besides the regular classes the student is attending. Sometimes disabled students do need special classes in order to get a good education. In such cases, however, whenever it is possible, disabled students should spend at least part of their day with non-handicapped students, for example at recess or in the library.

How can a student who wants special-education services get them?

In order to find out whether you need special-education services, you must be evaluated by experts paid for by the school. You can be referred to an expert for evaluation by your parent, or by a teacher or other school official, or by an outside person such as a social worker with a parent's consent. If the experts decide that you need special education, the school and your parents must prepare an "Individualized Education Program" for you. This IEP describes exactly what special services or programs the school will provide to you. Older students can and should participate in making their own IEP. Disabled students have the right to participate in extracurricular activities and gym classes unless their IEP says they cannot, although the school may not have to provide every activity to disabled children that it provides to children without disabilities.

If you are unhappy with a special-education evaluation or program, you or your parents have the right to request a hearing before a person who does not work for the school district. You are entitled to have a lawyer at the hearing and to appeal the decision of the hearing officer to a court if you do not like the decision.

4

THE FIRST AMENDMENT: FREEDOM OF EXPRESSION

Congress shall make no law . . . abridging the freedom of speech, or of the press; or the right of the people peaceably to assemble, and to petition the government for a redress of grievances.

—from the First Amendment, United States Constitution

Probably the most important rights we have as Americans are those guaranteed by the First Amendment to the Constitution: the rights to speak and to write and to assemble peaceably, to express our views without fear that the government will punish us for our opinions. In this book, we refer to all these rights together as the right to free expression. The reason these rights of free expression are so important is that they form the basis for our other rights. If we cannot talk freely about the problems and issues that affect our lives, we can never change anything that is wrong. For example, segregation in the public schools would never have been abolished if people had not been permitted to speak and write and demonstrate against it.

Do students have the right to express their opinions on any subject while they are in school?

Yes. The right to free expression is just as important for young people as it is for adults. Students have the same interest that adults have in expressing opinions on political issues such as the environment, race and sex discrimination, foreign policy, and local and national elections. In addition, since almost all young people between the ages of five and eighteen spend nearly half of their waking hours during most of the year in and around school, they also have a substantial interest in expressing their opinions about school-related issues. It is therefore very important that students be permitted and encouraged to debate freely their views on controversial issues while they are at school. In the words of the Supreme Court, "It is . . . this kind of openness . . . that is the basis of our National strength and of the independence and vigor of Americans."

On the other hand, the main job of the public schools is to educate the students who are required to attend them. Obviously, if school officials could place no limitations at all on the right of students to engage in First Amendment activities, such as speaking and distributing literature and demonstrating while they are in school, the schools would be unable to accomplish their job of providing young people with an education. Therefore, although students do not, as the Supreme Court put it, "shed their constitutional rights to freedom of speech or expression at the schoolhouse gate," school officials may place reasonable limits on those rights when their exercise is inconsistent with education.

What limits may schools place on student expression?

The Supreme Court has decided three cases involving the First Amendment rights of public-school students in different situations. These cases establish the basic principles that school

27

officials must apply when balancing the First Amendment rights of students against the educational mission of the school.

POLITICAL EXPRESSION: THE *TINKER* DECISION

The first student free-speech case, which was decided by the Supreme Court in 1969, is *Tinker v. Des Moines Independent Community School District*.[1] The case began in December 1965, when Mary Beth Tinker, a thirteen-year-old, junior-high-school student; her fifteen-year-old brother John; and sixteen-year-old Christopher Eckhardt, joined a group of adults and other students who were opposed to the war in Vietnam. The group decided to publicize its views on the war by wearing black armbands during the holiday season. The principals of the Des Moines, Iowa, schools that Mary Beth, John, and Christopher attended became aware of their plan to wear armbands. The principals announced that any student who wore an armband to school would be asked to remove it, and if the student refused, he or she would be suspended until agreeing to return without the armband. All three students wore their armbands to school and were suspended. They refused to return to school until after New Year's Day, when their protest was scheduled to end.

The students' fathers filed a lawsuit on their behalf in federal district court. The students asked the court to declare that they had a First Amendment right to express their views about the war by wearing armbands to school, and to order the school officials not to punish them for having done so. The federal court, however, upheld the principals' right to prohibit the armbands. The students appealed to the Court of Appeals for the Eighth Circuit, which affirmed the district court's decision. The students then petitioned the Supreme Court to hear the case, and the Court agreed to do so.

The Supreme Court found that the decisions of the lower courts had been incorrect. It held that students may not be prevented from exercising their First Amendment rights to free expression unless by doing so they "materially and substantially disrupt the work and discipline of the school." Since the armbands worn by Mary Beth, John, and Christopher were not disruptive, the students should not have been prohibited from wearing them.

VULGAR AND INDECENT EXPRESSION: THE *FRASER* DECISION

In 1986, the Supreme Court decided the second case involving students' First Amendment rights, *Bethel School District No. 403 v. Fraser*.[2] There the Court held that school officials have the right to censor student speech that is vulgar or indecent even if it does not cause a material or substantial disruption of the work or discipline of the school. The plaintiff in the case was Matthew Fraser, a high-school honor student who was suspended after he delivered a nominating speech at a school assembly for a fellow student who was running for student council. In the speech Matthew used language that school officials found vulgar and indecent. The speech was described by the Supreme Court as "an elaborate, graphic, and explicit sexual metaphor."

The Supreme Court upheld the suspension, emphasizing the facts that the assembly at which the speech was delivered was compulsory; that the audience consisted mainly of fourteen-year-olds, many of whom yelled and hooted and made hand gestures in response to the speech; and that two teachers had told Matthew ahead of time not to deliver it. The Court held that although the speech did not cause a material and substantial disruption, schools have an "interest in teaching students the boundaries of socially appropriate behavior."

Therefore, school officials have a very good educational reason for prohibiting students from using "vulgar and offensive terms in public discourse." Lower courts that have decided similar cases since the *Fraser* decision have disagreed about whether the decision means that school officials may censor all vulgar student speech or only vulgar speech that occurs at a school-sponsored event like the assembly in *Fraser* or in a school-sponsored publication.

SCHOOL-SPONSORED EXPRESSION: THE *KUHLMEIER* DECISION

The final important First Amendment case involving students is *Hazelwood School District v. Kuhlmeier*, decided in 1988.[3] In that case, school officials censored articles in the school newspaper concerning the experiences of several students with pregnancy and with divorces in their families. The Supreme Court upheld the censorship, ruling that school officials have the power to control the content of student publications that are paid for by the school, as long as the officials' actions "are reasonably related to legitimate pedagogical concerns"—in other words, as long as the officials have a good educational reason for censoring the material.

In the opinion of the Supreme Court, one legitimate concern of school officials is that readers not be exposed to material that may be inappropriate for their age level. In *Kuhlmeier*, the school principal said that the article's references to sexual activity and birth control were inappropriate for some of the younger students at the school. Therefore, the Court found, the principal had behaved appropriately in censoring the article. School officials may also censor speech that is part of the school curriculum on the grounds that it is biased, poorly written, or vulgar, because these are all good educational reasons.

The *Kuhlmeier* decision does *not*, however, give school officials the right to censor school-sponsored student speech simply because they disagree with its point of view. Thus, for example, school officials may censor all articles about sexuality and birth control because they believe that the entire topic is inappropriate for young teenagers. But they cannot censor an article advocating sex-education classes in school if they have agreed to publish another article opposing such classes.

When you put the three Supreme Court cases together, you can find the general principles that you should apply when you are trying to determine what your First Amendment rights are in a particular situation.

1. School officials may not prevent students from expressing their personal views while they are at school, as long as in doing so the students do not cause a material and substantial disruption in the work and discipline of the school (*Tinker*).

2. School officials may place limits on student speech that is sponsored by the school—for example, in a school-financed newspaper or a classroom assignment—as long as they have a good educational reason for doing so and not simply because they disagree with the student's point of view (*Kuhlmeier*).

3. School officials can forbid students to express their views in vulgar or indecent language (*Fraser*). Lower courts disagree about whether this rule applies to all student speech or only to school-sponsored speech.

When can schools limit student expression because it is disruptive?

In discussing material and substantial disruption, the Supreme Court emphasized the difference between a disruption caused by an idea that upsets people, and a disruption caused by the time or place or manner in which the idea is expressed. For example, while students may be encouraged to cheer and wave signs in support of the school team at a basketball game in the school gym, the identical cheer and sign could be prohibited in the school library. Few people might dispute the opinion that the school team is terrific, but most would agree that the library is not the place to express that opinion at top volume.

In contrast, the school officials in *Tinker*, for example, never claimed that armbands in general are disruptive. Rather, they testified that they were afraid that disruption would be caused by the opinion expressed by the particular armband: the opinion that the Vietnam war was wrong. The First Amendment does not prohibit reasonable restrictions on the time, place, or manner in which opinions may be expressed. It does, however, almost always prohibit restrictions on the ideas expressed in those opinions.

Can schools limit the time, place, and manner of student speech?

Under the *Tinker* "material and substantial disruption" test, school officials have great discretion in making reasonable rules that govern the time, place, and manner in which students may express their views while they are in school. For example, students can certainly be forbidden to engage in most free-speech activities while class is going on, since obviously the expression of personal views at that time and in that place could disrupt the work and discipline of the school. Whether students may be prohibited from engaging in First Amendment activities outside of the classroom depends on the precise nature of the activity (for example, handing out leaflets, as opposed to holding a rally), the exact time (before or after school, at lunch, or between classes), and the precise nature of the place (for example, in a narrow crowded hall or a spacious lobby). In cases challenging particular time, place, and manner restrictions, courts have upheld restrictions on distribution of literature in school hallways and near a school entrance.

Keep in mind that any time, place, and manner restrictions on expression must be reasonable. A blanket rule against handing out literature anywhere at any time inside a school has been declared unreasonable and therefore illegal by some courts. Likewise, a rule that restricts distribution of literature to a time and place that prevents most students from getting it is also unreasonable. As one court said, "By excluding the period when the vast majority of the desired audience will be present and available for communication, the restriction is in effect a prohibition. The First Amendment includes the right to receive as well as to disseminate information."

Keep in mind, too, that the *Tinker* test permits school officials to limit students' First Amendment activities only if the disruption they cause is "material and substantial." This means that a little bit of disruption caused by students' expression of their views does not justify prohibiting that expression completely. For example, in one case in which school officials prohibited students from handing out a school newspaper because they were being disruptive, the court said that it was the students' "misconduct in the manner in which they distributed the paper which should have been stopped, not the idea of printing newspapers itself."

The same court explained that sometimes schools must put up with minor disruptions when students exercise their First Amendment rights. Since the "interruption of class periods caused by the 'newspaper' were minor and few in number," the court said, the *Tinker* standard of material and substantial disruption had not been met.

In contrast, another court refused to permit students to wear buttons because those handing out the buttons were being noisy and were stopping other students in the hall. A better solution might have been to stop the disruptive behavior rather than prohibiting the buttons.

Can schools restrict the content of student speech?

Usually not. School officials have far less power to restrict the content of student expression than they have to impose restrictions on the time, place, or manner of such expression. This is true even if the ideas being expressed upset people. As the Supreme Court said in *Tinker*, "Any word, spoken, in class, in the lunchroom, or on the campus, that deviates from the views of another person may start an argument or cause a disturbance." The Court went on to point out, however, that "freedom of expression would not truly exist if the right could be exercised only in an area that a benevolent government has provided as a safe haven for crackpots."

Sometimes, school authorities try to prevent students from peacefully expressing controversial views because other students who disagree with them have become boisterous and disruptive. When a speaker is prohibited from expressing his or her views because the authorities fear that listeners will become hostile, that audience has exercised what is called the "heckler's veto." Courts have consistently held that, except in situations in which there is a "clear and present danger" of violence, a speaker may not be silenced because of the reactions of the audience to the speech. This makes sense because if it were not the law, anyone who disagreed with a speaker's opinions could prevent her or him from expressing them just by causing a disruption during the speech.

Applying this rule in the context of a school, at least one court has held that school officials should not have attempted to ban distribution of a student newspaper because it contained views that were likely to offend other students. The court said that if the student distributed the newspaper in an "orderly, non-disruptive manner, then he should not suffer if other students, who are lacking in self-control, tend to over-react, thereby becoming a disruptive influence."

Are there any times when the content of student speech can be restricted?

Yes. Sometimes if tensions among students at a school are very high, then some limitations on students' right to free expression of their views may be permitted because of the fear of other students' reactions. In such circumstances, school officials have the duty to take all reasonable steps to control disruptive students, rather than simply to prohibit speech. One Texas court, for example, in a case in which the school superintendent had barred the wearing of armbands because of rumors of planned disruptions, warned school officials not to base their fear of disruption simply on "intuition" that something bad might happen. The court said, "We believe that the Supreme Court [in *Tinker*] has declared a constitutional right which school authorities must nurture and protect, not extinguish, unless they find the circumstances allow them no practical alternative." Nevertheless, in another case, a court ruled that the use of the name "Rebels" and of the Confederate flag as the symbols of a school that had recently been desegregated could be prohibited in light of the serious problem of racial violence at the school at that time. The court said, however, that the prohibition could not be permanent but should last only as long as it was absolutely necessary to prevent disruption.

How have courts applied the "material and substantial disruption" test?

After the Supreme Court ruled that students could be prohibited from expressing their views only if they caused a material and substantial disruption, students from around the country brought lawsuits in which they argued that school officials had violated their First Amendment rights. It then became the job of the lower courts to examine the facts in these cases and to determine whether the school officials had acted appropriately. A look in the following pages at some of these cases will give you an idea of how courts have applied the "material and substantial disruption" test in a variety of situations. Keep in mind that courts in different parts of the country do not always agree with each other.

Can students be prohibited from wearing buttons, armbands, or clothing bearing messages?

No, usually not. Students can rarely be prohibited from wearing buttons, armbands, or clothing that have symbols or words printed on them because, as the Supreme Court's decision in *Tinker* shows, such articles are not disruptive in and of themselves. Thus, unless the words or symbols are vulgar or indecent (this is discussed later in the chapter), the only reason school officials could have for prohibiting them would be because the message they convey is likely to cause a substantial disruption that cannot be controlled in any other manner. In one case, students sued school officials who had prohibited them from wearing buttons bearing the word "scab" with a line drawn through it during a teachers' strike. The court found that the word "scab" was not vulgar or lewd or plainly offensive and that it therefore could not be suppressed unless school officials could reasonably predict that it would cause a material or substantial disruption, which the court found that they could not.

Can buttons, armbands, or clothing ever be found disruptive?

Yes, although a situation in which a button will be found disrup-

tive is very unusual. For example, a court upheld school officials who refused to permit students to wear buttons because
in the past, students had worn racially inflammatory buttons
that had caused tensions and disruptions at the school. Similarly, another court upheld a school principal's ban on the wearing
of armbands bearing the words "strike," "rally," and "stop the
killing" just after the United States invaded Cambodia during
the Vietnam War and four students who were protesting the
invasion at Kent State University were killed by National Guards-
men. The court found that the students disagreed strongly
about these issues and that disruption was so likely that a temporary ban on certain kinds of armbands was justified.

In a different kind of case, one court has found that a
school dress code prohibiting clothing that advertises alcohol
beverages is not unconstitutional. The court found that the
school board that instituted the dress code could reasonably
predict that allowing students to wear clothing advertising
alcoholic beverages would encourage consumption of alcohol
before or during school, as well as encouraging discussion of
alcohol which would substantially disrupt or interfere with
classwork and the discipline of the school.

Do students have the right to distribute non–school-sponsored literature in school?

Yes, with some limits. Obviously, the distribution of literature
such as underground newspapers or leaflets or religious tracts
has far greater potential for disrupting the work and discipline
of a school than does the wearing of buttons or armbands.
Nevertheless, a school may not pass a blanket regulation prohibiting the distribution of literature, nor can it pass a general
rule prohibiting disruptive literature and then decide later
what is disruptive. Any rule limiting the distribution of literature by students in school must be very specific to comply with

the demands of the First Amendment. For example, one federal court has held that a school rule prohibiting distribution of literature that could "reasonably lead the principal to forecast substantial disruption of or material interference with school activities" was too vague, even though it used the language from *Tinker*. The court explained that the rule was too vague because it gave no definition of the words "substantial disruption" or "material interference." This meant that a disruption was simply whatever the principal said it was. Also, the rule did not establish the criteria for predicting when literature would be likely to cause a disruption, such as recent disruptions about the same issue at the school.

There are cases in which courts have permitted school administrators to prohibit distribution of literature in specific emergency situations where there was a reason to believe that violence was about to occur. In one case, for example, school officials took signs away from a student who was passing them out on the day of a planned walkout from a school athletic-awards ceremony. The court found that in light of the generally tense atmosphere in the school caused by the announced walkout and rumors that the athletes scheduled to receive the awards planned to use physical force to stop anyone from leaving the ceremony, the school officials' fear of violence was reasonable. Therefore they were justified in taking the signs. The court went on to hold, however, that while school officials acted properly in taking the signs in an emergency, they should not have suspended from school the student who was passing them out.

In another case, students in an Illinois high school produced a newspaper urging their classmates to throw away some materials that were given them by the school staff to take to their parents. A federal appeals court said that the publication was protected by the First Amendment, since there was no evidence from which school officials could reasonably have predicted that the newspaper would cause a substantial disruption of school activity. This was so because the students were not rallying their classmates to disrupt the school immediately. If they had been doing so, however, the situation might have required emergency action. Two other federal courts have taken the same position. One declared invalid a school regulation prohibiting any publication that urges people to commit illegal actions or to disobey school rules for student conduct. The other court found unconstitutional a school-board policy prohibiting distribution of any publication that "advocates illegal actions, or is grossly insulting to any group or individual."

Can students hand out literature criticizing the school?

Yes. In some cases, school officials have prohibited students from criticizing school policies or school employees because they say it will undermine discipline among students. Courts, however, have held that students' criticism of their school is protected by the First Amendment, unless school officials can produce specific evidence that discipline will be undermined. For example, in one case a school tried to ban a newspaper written by students off campus that contained an article suggesting that the dean had a "sick mind." The court found that the remark was "disrespectful and tasteless," but that it could not be banned because it did not cause a material or substantial disruption.

Can school officials prohibit students from distributing literature on the ground that it is libelous?

Sometimes a school official will try to ban an article in a student newspaper because it is libelous. The Supreme Court has held that libel is printing something about a person that you know, or should know, is not true, in order to damage the per-

39

son's reputation. Slander is the oral version of such writings. If what you write is libelous, you can be sued for money damages. If your criticism is about a school official and you have good reason to believe that what you say is true, your statements are not libelous, even if it turns out that they are not true. If you say something that is true, it cannot be libelous. This is the standard in cases that do not involve student publications, and at least one federal court has held that the same standard applies to student publications. Therefore, it struck down a school rule that prohibited the publication of "libelous" material in a school newspaper because the definition of libel used by the school was different from that of the Supreme Court.

Can students be prohibited from expressing their views if both sides of a controversy are banned?

Some school officials seem to think that students may be prohibited from expressing their views on controversial subjects as long as "both sides" are banned. While school officials who make such rules may be trying to be fair, the *Tinker* decision makes clear that school officials may not prohibit students from expressing their views because they are afraid that controversy will disrupt education.

In one case, a school district prohibited a student from handing out leaflets seeking volunteers to work for the Democratic presidential candidate. The school said that it had a rule prohibiting the use of school facilities for all political activities on one side or the other of a particular issue, including activities on behalf of both major political parties. A federal court ruled that this policy violated the students' First Amendment rights, even though Republican students would be subject to the same rule.

Likewise, several federal courts have declared unconstitutional laws and regulations prohibiting the distribution on school property of all religious material or of any material that had a "sectarian, partisan, or denominational character" or had the purpose of "spread[ing] propaganda." Still another federal court held unconstitutional a school rule that prohibited recruitment among the students by any organization of "political/partisan and/or religious sectarian character within the school." Again, the fact that no political or religious group at all could recruit students in school did not make the rule constitutional. One court, however, has upheld a rule prohibiting students from distributing more than ten copies of written material primarily prepared by non-students. The court accepted as valid school officials' reason for the rule: that it was intended to encourage students to write their own material, rather than distributing the words of others.

Of course, in any situation in which a school is not required to allow students to engage in First Amendment activities, but nevertheless decides to do so, it must give equal opportunity to students on different sides of an issue to express their views. For example, although a school might have the right to prohibit students from setting up literature tables in the school lobby, it would not have the right to allow students to distribute anti-abortion literature while prohibiting pro-choice students from handing out their leaflets.

Can students sell literature at school?

Courts have disagreed on the question of whether students can sell literature on school grounds, rather than just give it away. One federal court ruled that students could not be barred from selling literature or selling space for advertisements, unless under the *Tinker* test there was evidence of disruption. A second court, however, upheld a prohibition against selling any product, including political literature, on school property. This decision seems to be inconsistent with the rule in *Tinker*. It would definitely be illegal to prohibit you from selling your literature if other student literature such as the official school newspaper can be sold.

In another case, a school had a rule that prohibited handing out commercial advertisements and soliciting money on school premises. Students who wanted to hand out an underground newspaper that contained ads and requests for contributions to support itself challenged the rule in court. The court upheld the general rule, but said that it could not be applied to the newspaper in question. It pointed out that the school itself subscribed to many magazines that contained ads, and it found that "the dissemination of commercial advertisements within a publication devoted largely to expression of opinion and factual matter can scarcely be said to be an evil which, standing by itself, is in need of elimination." In two other cases where courts upheld students' right to distribute underground newspapers on school property, the papers were either sold or contributions were solicited.

Can students be required to show their literature to school officials before distributing it?

Probably. Sometimes schools have rules requiring students to show their literature to school officials before passing it out. Outside of school, the First Amendment prohibits "prior restraints" on free speech. This means that while in rare instances people may be punished for expressing their views after they have expressed them, they cannot be stopped from expressing them in the first place. For example, a magazine that publishes libel may be sued after the magazine comes out, but the government cannot seize all copies of the magazine to prevent the magazine from ever reaching the newsstands.

Courts have disagreed about whether the general rule

prohibiting prior restraints applies in schools. Two federal appeals courts have held that no prior approval of student publications can be required, since this rule would violate the prior-restraints rule. Other courts, however, have permitted school officials to determine in advance whether the distribution of a particular piece of literature will materially and substantially disrupt the school. These courts have required that the school adopt specific rules that clearly state exactly which literature must be submitted in advance and to whom it must be submitted.

Also, the school must give a definite and brief time within which a decision has to be made about whether a piece of literature may be distributed. A federal court in California that approved a rule requiring prior approval of student literature emphasized the need for a quick decision. It warned that where the literature is "political or social, and the effectiveness of the item may be severely diminished by even a brief delay in its distribution, it may be that even one day's restraint is an impermissible burden." Therefore, if for example you have to submit to the principal for her or his approval a leaflet announcing a rally the next afternoon, you have a very strong argument for requiring a decision the same day.

Finally, the school may be required to provide an opportunity for the students to present their point of view at a hearing. If a decision is made that they may not pass out their literature, students must be given an opportunity to appeal that decision quickly to higher school authorities.

Can students solicit funds for specialized causes at school?

Maybe. Sometimes students want to solicit money on school grounds to support political or social or charitable causes. Raising money to support causes in which one believes has long been held to be a protected activity under the First Amendment. Therefore, the *Tinker* test of material and substantial disruption ought to apply to this kind of activity. The one court that directly considered the issue, however, denied students the right to distribute flyers soliciting funds for the defense of a political trial; the court feared that many groups might put pressure on students to raise money for them.

If you want to distribute literature or solicit money for a cause you support, you should consider ahead of time how you can avoid causing the material and substantial disruption that will permit school officials to prohibit you from doing so. It is always better to avoid the problem in the first place than to fight about it after your literature has been confiscated and you have been punished. Consider the following examples:

1. Leaflets in the classroom. Certainly you have no right to pass out leaflets or other literature in the classroom while class is going on, and perhaps not before class either, since this activity might interfere with students' getting to their seats and preparing for class.

2. Leaflets in the halls. Although this would not directly interfere with classes, you might substantially interfere with traffic in the halls and delay students from getting to class on time, especially in schools with narrow, crowded halls. A court applying the *Tinker* test might, therefore, find that handing out leaflets in halls could legally be prohibited.

3. Setting up a literature table in the lobby. If it is a small lobby and the table or the students gathering around it clog up the space, you would have the same problem as with the halls. On the other hand, if it is a large lobby and there is no substantial interference with students' passing through, and if you are not supposed to be in class or study period, a court would likely find that you have the right to set up a table. Your case would be stronger if you could show that tables were set up there for other purposes—for example, for the student government to sell prom tickets or for the PTA to have a bake sale. After all, if their tables are not substantially disruptive, then yours would not be either.

If a school official tries to stop you because students are taking away your literature and throwing it on the floor, you should suggest that those persons be punished for littering rather than stopping your speech. That is how the law works when leaflets are being passed out on the street. You should point out that if the school stops you from handing out literature because other students throw it on the floor, it will be very easy for students who disagree with you to take your literature and litter the school and thus keep you from expressing your views. As a practical matter, you could also make sure that you have a litter basket near your table and you could offer to help pick up discarded leaflets.

Can students hold demonstrations at school?

Probably not. The First Amendment protects "peaceable assembly"; this means that the government may not prohibit people from marching or demonstrating in public places to express their views. Although public school property is owned by the government, it is obviously not the same as a public street or park. Rather, a school is what is called a "limited public forum" which means that it is a place that is open to the public for a particular purpose—the education of students. Therefore, school officials are permitted to prohibit First Amendment activities on school property that prevent the school from carrying out its purpose, or, in other words, activities that materially and substantially disrupt its functioning.

When it comes to demonstrations on school property, most court decisions have been unfavorable to students who wish to demonstrate, particularly when the demonstration takes place during school hours or inside a school building, because such demonstrations are likely materially and substantially to disrupt school activities. One court, for example, upheld the suspension of African-American students who walked out of a school pep rally when the song "Dixie" was played. School officials had found the walkout disruptive. In another case, a federal court held that students could be suspended for staying out of school and conducting a rally to protest school policies that they claimed were racially discriminatory. One court even permitted a school to ban *all* demonstrations inside any school building. It simply assumed that any indoor demonstration would be disruptive.

Another court dealt with demonstrations in school buildings in a different way. It held that a student sit-in could not be prohibited simply because it was inside a school building or because other students gathered in the halls to watch, or because school officials who chose to watch the demonstration could not attend to their regular duties. The court said that in deciding whether a particular demonstration materially or substantially interferes with school activities, a court must look only at the behavior of the protesters themselves, not of the audience. In this case, the court did uphold the suspensions of the protesting students from school, but that was because the demonstrators themselves missed class and made so much noise that some classes had to be moved to other places and others were disturbed.

Can students hold demonstrations outside of a school?

A demonstration outside of a school building has more chance of being found legal than one inside a building, because an outside demonstration is less likely to materially and substantially disrupt the school than an inside one. Some courts have therefore held that a rule banning all demonstrations on school property is not constitutional since some orderly and peaceful demonstrations will not materially and substantially disrupt school activities. A federal court in Puerto Rico also held that a rule that prohibited demonstrations that "affected the institutional order" was too vague to be constitutional. The court said that school officials would have to make more specific rules describing the disruptive conduct before they could constitutionally enforce such a rule.

From these cases it is clear that for two reasons, demonstrations during school hours are more likely to be held illegal than those held before or after school. First, they are more likely to disrupt classes, and second, the demonstrators themselves will be absent from classes. However, if you participate in a demonstration during school and miss classes, you cannot be punished more severely than students who skip classes without permission for other reasons, because that would be punishing you for expressing your ideas rather than for skipping class.

Finally, whether your demonstration is inside or outside on school property, a court is more likely to find the action legal if it concerns school policies rather than national issues. While a court may not agree with you that a school is a proper place to protest against foreign policy, it might agree that it is the only effective place to protest a school dress code.

Do students have the right to form clubs and organizations at school?

Yes. The First Amendment protects the right to form groups and associations for the purpose of the expression of ideas. Therefore, applying the rule in *Tinker*, students have the right to form after-school clubs to discuss controversial issues and express unpopular views, unless the school can show that the club "materially and substantially" disrupts school activities.

One school, for example, had a policy forbidding students to form clubs with a "partisan" point of view (that means a club whose members want to express only one side of a particular issue) and therefore would not allow students to form a chapter of an antiwar organization called the Student Mobilization Committee. A court overruled the school administration, saying, as the Supreme Court did in *Tinker*, that participating in the organization would not disrupt the school and indeed would teach students a great deal. In another case, the Supreme Court ruled that a college could not deny official recognition to a chapter of a student political organization called Students for a Democratic Society unless the school could show that the goal of the organization was to disrupt the school. In a similar case involving high-school students, a federal court ruled that "absent a threat to the orderly operation of the school, to deny recognition to a student group for the reason that it advocates 'controversial' ideas is unconstitutional." Another court ordered the administrators of a state college to register a gay students' organization and to give it all of the privileges that other student organizations had, such as the use of the university's facilities and funding.

A number of schools have prohibited students from forming religious clubs. Courts have held such rules to be unconstitutional, saying that religious clubs must be treated the same as other types of clubs. This is discussed in the next chapter.

If a school generally permits clubs to select their own programs and to invite outside speakers, then students cannot be prohibited from inviting a speaker unless school officials can show that the speaker is likely to create disorder at the school. As is the case with the actions of students themselves, the school's fear of disorder cannot be based on speculation. Rather, the school must have clear and convincing evidence that the speaker will cause a disruption at the school.

Do students have the right to hold social events at school?

Yes. The First Amendment right of freedom of association does not simply protect students' right to associate with one another to discuss important issues. It also protects students' right to socialize with whomever they please. One court, for example, ruled that a gay students' organization could not be prohibited from holding a dance. School officials argued that although the organization could hold meetings to discuss issues, a dance was not protected by the First Amendment. The court disagreed, pointing out that social events can play an "important role . . . in individuals' efforts to associate and further their common beliefs." On this reasoning, too, gay students must be permitted to invite partners of the same sex to social events such as proms.

At least one court, however, has upheld a rule prohibiting students from attending parties where alcohol is served. The court rejected a student's argument that the rule violated her First Amendment right of free association, saying that that right was outweighed by the school board's interest in deterring alcohol consumption by students.

Do students have the right to use school facilities to express their views?

Sometimes. Often students want to use school facilities such as bulletin boards, loudspeakers, copier machines, or meeting rooms to aid them in expressing their views. The school is not required to allow students to use its facilities for the expression of their personal views. But if it lets one group of students do so, it must also allow students to express opposing views, because the government is not allowed to favor one side in a debate by denying the other side the ability to express its opinion.

For example, one court held that it was unconstitutional

for school officials to refuse to distribute notices informing parents of a rally in favor of busing students to different schools to achieve racial integration, when those officials had agreed to distribute notices to parents about antibusing rallies. Another example is a case in which an antiwar organization had been denied permission by the school board to provide students with information regarding legal alternatives to the draft and military service, even though representatives of the armed services were permitted to provide students with information about military careers. The court declared that the school's action was unconstitutional because it favored one point of view, and ordered that the antiwar organization be given the same access to students and school facilities as was given to military recruiters.

A court might require a school to let students use a school bulletin board, since a notice on a bulletin board is unlikely to be disruptive. A school might legitimately reserve a particular bulletin board for official school announcements, but a court is not likely to uphold a school's right to deny students any space at all for the expression of student views. If some students take down other students' announcements, school officials have the obligation to take action against the students who are attempting to suppress the views of others, rather than banning student use of school bulletin boards.

May school officials censor student speech in publications that the school pays for?

Usually yes. As discussed earlier, the Supreme Court has held in the *Kuhlmeier* case that school officials have great discretion to control the content of school-sponsored student speech for educational reasons. Educational reasons include the determination that a subject matter is not appropriate for students to read about. Educational reasons also include the conclusion that particular articles are rude, insulting, vulgar, obscene, libelous, biased, badly written, ungrammatical, or factually incorrect. School officials are not, however, permitted to censor even school-sponsored speech simply because they disagree with your point of view.

In many cases, of course, students and school officials may disagree about whether an article is any of the above things or whether the school official simply does not agree with the viewpoint. For example, in one case, school officials disqualified a student from running for student counsel after he made what the officials believed were rude remarks about the school's assistant principal at a school-sponsored assembly. In his speech the student said,

> *"The administration plays tricks with your mind and they hope you won't notice. For example, why does Mr. Davidson stutter while he is on the intercom? He doesn't have a speech impediment. If you want to break the iron grip of this school, vote for me for president. I can try to bring back student rights that you have missed and maybe get things that you have always wanted. All you have to do is vote for me, Dean Poling."*

The court that considered the case concluded that it was not irrational for school authorities to take offense at a remark that was calculated to get Dean Poling votes at the expense of the assistant principal's dignity. The court held that civility is a legitimate educational concern and that the school officials therefore did not violate the student's First Amendment rights when they punished him.

It is worth noting that one judge dissented in the case on the grounds that Dean Poling's speech was "political speech pure and simple," not a vulgar one like the speech found unprotected in the *Fraser* case or one that caused any disrup-

51

tion. Thus, the school officials were really punishing him for his point of view. The dissenting judge ended his opinion by asking, "If the school administration can silence a student criticizing it for being narrow minded and authoritarian, how can students engage in political dialog with their educators about their education?"

This is a very good question and it illustrates the need for the First Amendment. Nevertheless, the law is clear that when a school sponsors speech by paying for a publication or holding an assembly, and where the speech may therefore appear to have the approval of the school, the school has the right to censor it. Courts almost invariably resolve disputes between school administrators and students concerning such censorship in favor of the school administrators. In the words of one court which upheld the right of school officials to prohibit ads from Planned Parenthood in high-school newspapers, yearbooks, and programs at athletic events, "A school's decision not to promote or sponsor speech that is unsuitable for immature audiences, or which might place it on one side of a controversial issue, is a judgment call which *Kuhlmeier* reposes in the discretion of school officials and which is afforded substantial deference."

How can students avoid school censorship?

If you wish to avoid censorship of articles about your school, your best bet is to avoid using language that will give school officials a good reason for censoring you. If you think it is necessary to use language that school officials might consider vulgar, you might try to explain why the particular language is essential to the point you are trying to make. As one federal judge noted, "Critics of the established order have frequently found it necessary to use language that shocked their audiences—neither Ezekiel nor Martin Luther spoke in bland terms." It would also be helpful to point out that many books and articles in the school library contain the same words to which the principal is objecting in student literature. One court, faced with such a situation, criticized school officials for their "rank inconsistency," which the court found "arbitrary and unreasonable."

Similarly, if you wish to write about controversial subjects in your school newspaper or put on controversial performances or assemblies, you must make an effort to show that students are already exposed to these topics in places such as school library books, local newspapers, counseling programs, or other activities in which students in that community engage. If editors can show that such subjects are generally considered suitable for high-school students in other situations, a school official will have less reason for censoring an article on the ground that it is unsuitable for students.

Do students have the right to use vulgar speech?

Usually not. As discussed above, the law is clear that school officials may censor school-sponsored speech that is vulgar or rude or indecent, since teaching the rules of "civilized discourse" is a legitimate educational concern. Some courts have gone even further and have upheld the actions of school officials in banning non–school-sponsored speech on these grounds. In one case, for example, a student was suspended from school for wearing a T-shirt bearing the words "Drugs Suck," which she had gotten at a rock concert. Although they agreed with the opinion the shirt expressed, school officials objected to the word "suck" on the grounds that in some contexts it has a sexual meaning and is therefore lewd and indecent. A federal court upheld the action of the school officials, despite the fact that no one could have believed that the school was responsible for the shirt and that it obviously simply expressed the views of the wearer. Instead of applying the *Tin-*

ker "material and substantial disruption" test, the court applied the reasoning in *Fraser* that the school has the right to teach students to use proper language.

Can school officials remove books from school libraries because they disagree with their content?

No. School officials often remove books from school libraries because they disapprove of the books' contents, but this practice is unconstitutional. In *Board of Education, Island Trees Union Free School District No. 26 v. Pico*,[4] the Supreme Court held that a school library provides "an environment especially appropriate for the recognition of the First Amendment rights of students." In that case, a school board had ordered the removal of nine books from school libraries in the district on the ground that the books were contrary to the values of the school-board members and of the community that they represented. The Supreme Court explained that while school officials have a great deal of power to make decisions about what books should be in their school libraries, they "may not remove books from school library shelves simply because they dislike the ideas contained in those books."

Despite this decision, the removal of books from school libraries and curricula is a problem that frequently arises. For example, in one case a federal court upheld the removal from the eleventh-grade curriculum of two great classics: *Lysistrata*, a play written by the Greek dramatist Aristophanes in 411 B.C., and *The Miller's Tale* written by the English poet Geoffrey Chaucer. The school officials disapproved of the sexual themes and vulgar language in the works, and the court held that this was a reason that under the *Kuhlmeier* decision justified the removal of books. This was true even though, as the court acknowledged, the books in question were important works of literature.

Another court has applied the same principle in a case in which school officials tried to prevent a grade-school class from performing a play that expressed ideas of which the officials disapproved. The court held that it was unconstitutional for school officials to stop the production solely because it did not approve of the play's content. This was particularly so since student participation was voluntary and the play was not part of the regular curriculum. The court quoted a Supreme Court justice in the *Island Trees* case who said that "allowing a school board to engage in such conduct hardly teaches children to respect the diversity of ideals that is fundamental to the American system."

Can students be forced to recite the Pledge of Allegiance?

No. The First Amendment not only prohibits the government from punishing you for expressing your views, it also prohibits the government from forcing you to express views that you do not hold. For this reason, students have challenged school rules forcing them to recite the Pledge of Allegiance to the flag. Flag-salute ceremonies are constitutional, but only as long as student participation is voluntary. The leading case on the flag salute was *West Virginia State Board of Education v. Barnette*,[5] involving children who were Jehovah's Witnesses suspended from school for refusing to salute the flag. They went to court and argued that reciting the pledge violated their religious beliefs and that forcing them to do so was unconstitutional. The Supreme Court agreed, holding that a compulsory flag salute in school violated students' right to free expression, "quite apart from their religious convictions."

Since the decision in *Barnette*, every court that has been faced with these cases has decided that students may remain quietly seated during the Pledge as long as they do not attempt to prevent others from saying it.

In one case, students in New York City remained seated and refused to recite the flag salute because they did not believe that the words of the Pledge were true in America today. In court, the school argued that other students had followed the example of the original students and were remaining seated. This fact did not disturb the court, which said, "The First Amendment protects successful dissent as well as ineffective protest." As to the fear of school officials that other students might become "infuriated" at those who sat, the court said, "The Constitution does not recognize fears of a disorderly reaction as ground for restricting peaceful expression." The court held that under the *Tinker* test, students had the right to remain quietly seated during the flag salute as a matter of conscience.

The next year, when some students in one of the same schools found themselves being harassed for remaining seated, the court issued a further order stating that the students could not be required to obtain parental permission in order to remain seated.

In one case, a student went to federal court to argue that not only should he be excused from reciting the Pledge of Allegiance, but that the school should not be permitted to hold flag-salute ceremonies at all. His reason was that the words "under God" in the Pledge turn it into a kind of prayer which schools are not permitted to sponsor. The court rejected this argument, holding that the words "under God" were ceremonial and not religious. Thus, the rule remains that schools may hold flag-salute ceremonies, but students may not be required to participate either by saying the words or by standing.

5

THE FIRST AMENDMENT: FREEDOM OF RELIGION

Congress shall make no law respecting an establishment of religion, or prohibiting the free exercise thereof.

—from the First Amendment, United States Constitution

What is the right to freedom of religion?

The First Amendment protects not only the right to free expression, it also protects the right to freedom of religion. This right has two parts. First, the government cannot interfere with the "free exercise" of religion. This means that it cannot tell anyone how to worship or whether to worship at all. Your religious beliefs and how you express them are entirely up to you. Second, the government may not "establish" a religion. That means that the government cannot favor one religion over another, or religion over no religion. In short, there must be a "separation of church and state."

Sometimes the right of free exercise of religion seems to

conflict with the prohibition against government establishment of religion. For example, if students want to say prayers at their school graduation, it may be hard to determine whether the school must let them do so in order to allow them to practice their religion freely, or whether it must forbid them from doing so to avoid government participation in religion. Many cases raise this issue.

Another problem arises when a school takes some action that could have either a religious purpose or a secular (non-religious) purpose. For example, in one case a student member of an extracurricular singing group objected to singing religious songs. She brought a lawsuit in which she argued that the school was violating the First Amendment by sponsoring the activity. The court, however, accepted the school's argument that a great deal of choral music happens to be religious and that the songs had been chosen for musical reasons, not religious ones. Therefore, since the school's purpose was not to teach religion, the court held that the school had not violated the First Amendment.

If you want to determine what your First Amendment religious rights are in school, keep in mind the following rules:

1. School officials cannot sponsor any religious activities such as prayer services or religious organizations.

2. School officials cannot prohibit students from engaging in religious activities—for example, private prayer or distribution of religious material.

3. Any actions that school officials take that involve religion must have a secular purpose. For example, school officials can place the same time, place, and manner restrictions on the distribution of religious literature as they can on any other kind of literature, because their purpose is simply to avoid disrupting students' education, not to prohibit them from practicing religion.

The issue of religion in the public schools is a subject about which many people feel strongly and about which they disagree. Therefore, there have been many lawsuits challenging various practices that involve religion in the public schools. Courts in these cases have often reached conflicting decisions. The Supreme Court has resolved some of these conflicts, but not all of them. Consequently, the law in the area is complicated and not always consistent.

Can students be required to say prayers in school?

No. The Supreme Court has held that the constitutional requirement that the government can play no part in religion means that schools may not conduct prayer services or Bible readings in school.[1] The Court has held that such religious exercises violate students' First Amendment right to freedom of religion, even if the prayers are nondenominational (not of any particular religion) and students' participation in them is voluntary. Such ceremonies are illegal even if students may be excused from attendance, because the government may not get involved with religion at all.

Can schools require a moment of silence instead of prayers?

No. Some states have passed laws requiring a voluntary moment of silence at the beginning of each school day. The Supreme Court held this to be unconstitutional, too, because the Court found that the reason the law had been passed was religious; the state was requiring the moment of silence as a substitute for prayers said aloud.[2] In a recent case, however, a federal court upheld a statute requiring a minute of silence at the beginning of each school day. The court did so because it accepted state officials' explanation that the statute had only the non-religious purpose of providing students with the opportunity for silent reflection on the activities of the day and was not for the religious purpose of returning prayers to schools.

Can school officials conduct prayers before athletic events?

No. Sometimes schools permit school employees such as team coaches to conduct prayers before games, practices, and other extracurricular activities. This practice is unconstitutional. While students themselves can certainly pray before a game, where a coach chooses a prayer, or decides when or where it will be recited, or leads the team or group in reciting it, the prayer is considered school-sponsored and therefore violates the First Amendment prohibition against establishment of religion.

Can prayers be recited at graduation ceremonies?

No. One of the most controversial questions concerning religion in public schools has been whether prayers are permitted at graduation ceremonies. The answer given to this question by the Supreme Court in 1992, in a case called *Lee v. Weisman*, is that a public school cannot constitutionally arrange for a member of the clergy to deliver a prayer at a graduation ceremony.[3] This is true even if the prayer is nondenominational—that is, not of any particular religion.

Since the decision in *Weisman*, there have been a number of cases in which schools have tried to get around the Supreme Court's decision by permitting students themselves to lead prayers at graduations when a majority of the students have voted to have them, instead of inviting a member of the clergy to conduct prayers. Courts have come to different conclusions on the constitutionality of this practice. One court has held that student-led and initiated prayers at graduation are constitutional as long as students themselves choose the content of the prayers, the prayers are nonsectarian, and their purpose is simply to solemnize the graduation, not to encourage religion. A majority of courts have held, however, that students' constitutional right to freedom of religion cannot be put to a majority vote. One such court pointed out that the graduating class had the authority to make the decision about graduation prayers only because the school allowed them to do so and that graduation was ultimately a school-related, school-sponsored event that must be kept free of religion.

Can students say prayers privately in school?

Yes. It is important to remember that a school cannot prevent an individual student from saying prayers privately in school. For example, if you want to say a prayer before a test or at the beginning of the day or at your graduation, you may do so. The school would be violating your right to freedom of religion to stop you. The Constitution simply prohibits school officials from leading your prayer.

Can schools permit released time for religious instruction?

Yes, some schools allow students to leave classes for religious instruction. Such programs have been found to be constitutional by the courts as long as students are not pressured to participate and the educational program of students who do not participate is not disrupted.[4]

Can schools display religious pictures and symbols, or use religious texts?

No. The Supreme Court has declared unconstitutional the practice of posting the Ten Commandments in classrooms, when the purpose of posting them is religious rather than educational.⁵ That is, if students were studying the religions of the world and the Ten Commandments were posted as an example of the kinds of things that people in certain religions believe, that would be educational and therefore constitutional. If, on the other hand, the Ten Commandments were posted because the school believed that students should obey them, that would be an impermissible religious purpose. In a similar case, another court permitted the display in classrooms of calendars showing holidays in different countries, including the holidays of the world's major religions. The court found that the secular purpose of the calendars was simply to teach students about the customs of other people and not to encourage religion. Another court found it unconstitutional for a school to place a picture of Jesus in a hall because the only purpose for the picture was religious.

Can students distribute religious literature at school?

The rules concerning distribution of student-produced religious literature in school are the same as those that apply to the distribution of non-religious student literature. School officials have the right to place reasonable time, place, and manner restrictions on the distribution of both kinds of literature. They have no right to censor a point of view.

Sometimes schools have prohibited the distribution of any literature that espouses a particular religion. These rules are unconstitutional, even though they apply equally to all religions, because they violate the Free Exercise Clause of the First Amendment.

Schools cannot, of course, sponsor religious speech or publications, because that would violate the Establishment Clause. In one case, a court found unconstitutional the practice of a school district of allowing members of the Gideon Society to come into classrooms to distribute Bibles. The court held that by giving class time to the group it was, in effect, sponsoring religion.

Can students form religious clubs and organizations at school?

Yes. Sometimes students want to hold religious meetings on school property outside of class time. If student groups are permitted to hold meetings on school property for other purposes, then religious students must be permitted to hold meetings for religious purposes. This right is specifically guaranteed by the Equal Access Act, a federal law.[6] The act, however, imposes some restrictions on religious meetings. First, the meetings must be organized by the students themselves and not by the school. Second, school staff may attend to insure discipline and safety of students, but they may not participate in the meeting. Finally, persons from outside the school, such as religious leaders, may not direct, conduct, control, or regularly attend such meetings.

Recently, a federal court held that a school rule prohibiting school clubs from discriminating against students on the basis of religion could be applied to a student-sponsored Christian Bible club. The students in the club objected to the rule as applied to them because it forced them to permit students who were not Christian to run for office. The students claimed that only Christians should be permitted to hold office in the club because each officer of the club "carrie[d] a significant spiritual responsibility and import." The court rejected this argument, ruling that for the school to permit students to discriminate against other students for a religious reason would be improperly sponsoring a particular religious belief.

6

PERSONAL APPEARANCE

**Can schools control the way students dress and
wear their hair?**

It depends. The way people choose to dress and wear their hair
is one of the most important ways of expressing their person-
alities. For example, if you see a young man wearing an earring
or baggy pants and a young woman wearing Doc Martens or
having dyed hair, you might make certain assumptions about
them, including what music they like and what their political
views are. (You might be wrong, of course, but you could often
make a good guess.) Thus, clothing sends messages, even
when it does not have anything written on it.

For this reason, many courts have held that the constitutional right to privacy, which is implied by several of the provisions in the Bill of Rights, and by the First Amendment
guarantee of free expression, protects our right to express our-
selves through clothing and hairstyles. These courts have concluded that public-school officials cannot tell students how to
dress or groom themselves, unless they can prove that the

clothing will cause a material and substantial disruption. This is true even if the dress code was written and adopted by the student body.

Many other courts, however, have disagreed that clothing and hairstyle choice is important enough to receive constitutional protection and have allowed schools to enforce dress codes without proving that the codes are necessary to avoid danger or prevent disruption in school. Thus, whether your school is allowed to make you dress or wear your hair a certain way may depend simply on what state you live in.

Even in the states in which schools are permitted to make rules for students' appearance, they are not required to do so. Therefore, many school districts have adopted rules similar to one in Pennsylvania which says,

> *Students have the right to govern the length or style of their hair including facial hair. Any limitations of this right shall include evidence that the length or style of hair causes a disruption of the educational process or constitutes a health or safety hazard. Where length or style of hair presents a problem some types of covering should be considered.*

While courts today generally uphold dress codes, they are sometimes more critical of rules that require students to cut their hair than they are of rules governing clothing. This is because hair rules necessarily affect students outside of school, while students can wear whatever they please after school.

Can particular clothing be banned because it indicates gang membership?

Yes. It seems odd now, given today's styles and attitudes about fashion, that the first lawsuits involving school dress codes generally challenged school rules that prohibited boys from

65

wearing long hair. Many schools also had rules requiring girls to wear skirts to school. In those days, it was very rare that school officials could produce evidence, in states in which they were required to do so, that a student's clothing was genuinely dangerous or disruptive. Today, however, many schools prohibit students from wearing certain articles of clothing that they believe are worn by members of gangs. Such clothing, the schools say, results in gang violence in schools. If school officials have strong evidence that particular clothing in fact results in violence, they have the right to prohibit students from wearing it. They should, however, have some proof that violence is likely, not simply that they are worried about it. As a practical matter, courts have almost always upheld anti-gang dress codes. One court, for example, upheld the prohibition on boys' wearing earrings, although the boy who brought the lawsuit had no connection with a gang. Likewise, another court found that a dress code prohibiting boys from wearing sagging pants was permissible. In that case the court rejected the student's First Amendment claim that wearing sagging pants was part of a hip-hop style which had African-American roots and therefore expressed his group identity.

Can students whose religion requires long hair be required to cut it?

No. One case in which a First Amendment claim was accepted by a court involved Native American boys who wished to wear their hair long, according to their people's tradition and, they claimed, as required by their religion. The court believed this claim and therefore required school officials to show that the boys' long hair disrupted the school. They were unable to show any disruption and the no–long-hair rule was struck down because the school's interest in the rule was outweighed by the students' interest in following their religion.

Can schools require students to wear uniforms?

The law is unclear. Some public schools are considering adopting uniforms to promote school discipline and spirit. Indeed, California now has a law that permits schools to require students to wear uniforms. This raises two separate issues. The first is whether a rule requiring a student to purchase a uniform violates the student's right to a free education. If uniforms are provided to students who cannot afford to buy them, that problem is solved. The other question is whether requiring a uniform violates the right to free expression. It probably would be difficult for school officials to prove that the failure of a student to wear a uniform would present a danger or disrupt the functioning of a school. That most students might want to wear a uniform does not mean that everyone must do so, since the Constitution protects individual rights and not the interests of the majority unless these are compelling.

No court has yet ruled whether school-uniform regulations are constitutional. The California law contains a provision allowing parents to decide that their children do not have to wear uniforms. A law containing such a provision is more likely to be constitutional than one that does not. On the other hand, it may also undermine the claim of school officials that the law is necessary to prevent gang violence.

7

SCHOOL DISCIPLINE AND DUE PROCESS

What is the right to "due process of law"?

The Constitution requires the government to treat all persons fairly. Specifically, the Fourteenth Amendment states that the government may not "deprive any person of life, liberty or property without due process of law." The principal, the teachers, the coaches, the school security guards, and any other employees of a public school are employees of the government. Therefore, the Supreme Court has held in a case called *Goss v. Lopez*,[1] that the Fourteenth Amendment requires them to treat you fairly. This means that they may not impose serious punishment because you did something wrong, without first having followed certain established procedures to determine if you are in fact guilty.

The right to due process also means that any punishment imposed must be in proportion to the offense committed. A serious punishment, such as expulsion from school, cannot be imposed on a student for a minor offense like chewing gum. Due process is also violated if a serious punishment is imposed on a student for doing something for which other students had received only minor punishment.

The right to due process only guarantees that you will be given a chance to show that you did not violate a school rule. A hearing will not determine whether the rule was a fair one in the first place. If, for example, your school has a rule against holding hands in the hall, the right to a hearing will not protect you if you and a friend were, in fact, holding hands. If you believe that a school rule is unfair, it is usually a bad idea to make your point by violating the rule and arguing at a hearing that the rule was unfair. In that situation, even if the school officials conclude that the rule *was* unfair and should be changed, they may still punish you for disobedience. It is far better to exercise your First Amendment rights and protest the rule as a law-abiding citizen than as the accused person at a disciplinary hearing.

What does the right to fair rules guarantee?

If you want to determine whether your school's regulations are reasonable, or if you want to convince your school officials to change rules that you do not think are fair, you might consider the recommendations of one state board of education:

1. The school must provide notice of what conduct is prohibited or permitted. A copy of the rules and procedures must be disseminated to all students.

2. School rules must be reasonably understandable to the average student.

3. The rules must be rationally related to a valid educational purpose.

4. The rules must be precise so as not to prohibit constitutionally protected activities.

5. The policy must provide students with notice of potential consequences for violating specific rules.

6. The type of punishment specified in the policy must be within the expressed or implied authority of the school district to utilize.

7. The punishment must be of reasonable severity in relation to the seriousness of the misconduct or the number of times the misconduct was committed.

Due-process rules may be different in different schools, but they should all contain these ideas. If they do not, then you may have a good argument that your school's rules are unfair. Let's see what these ideas mean.

"NOTICE OF PROHIBITED CONDUCT MUST BE PROVIDED"

Does a school have to put its rules in writing?

Not necessarily. An important requirement of due process is notice. This means that people must be informed of laws and rules so that they will know ahead of time what they are not allowed to do. You may have heard it said that "ignorance of the law is no defense." This simply means that if you are charged with breaking a law, you will not escape punishment by arguing that you did not know that there was such a law. This is true, however, only if the law has been published someplace where you could have found out about it if you had tried. If there was no way you could have known about the law, you would have a good argument that you had been deprived of your due-process right to notice. Many states require local school districts to put their school rules in writing. For example, one state does not allow a school to enforce a rule unless it has been published, approved by a school committee, filed with the state department of education, and provided free of charge to anyone who requests it.

Other school districts do not require written school disciplinary codes. A Texas court, for example, upheld student suspensions under a school rule that was not in writing. The court found that the rule had been announced at several school assemblies that the now-suspended students had attended. The court held that these announcements were enough to give students notice that the conduct was against the rules.

You can find out whether written rules are required in your school by writing to your state education department. Even if your school is not required to have written rules, you may not be punished for violating a policy you had no reason to believe existed, as opposed to one you could have known about had you bothered to do so. If, for example, you sometimes leave school during a free period instead of going to study hall, and students have never been told of a rule or policy that forbids students to leave the campus during the school day, it would be illegal to punish you. If, however, a teacher specifically tells you not to leave and you do, it is likely that you can be punished, even if there is no written rule forbidding you to do so. Just disobeying a school official is grounds for suspension in most school districts.

"RULES MUST BE REASONABLY UNDERSTANDABLE"

How specific do school rules have to be?

Sometimes even a written law or rule may be so unclear that, as the Supreme Court said in 1976, people "of common intelligence must necessarily guess at its meaning and differ as to its application." Such laws are "void for vagueness." That is, they are so vague that most people cannot understand exactly what they are not allowed to do. Moreover, vague laws are unconstitutional because they leave the decision about what conduct is prohibited up to the person who is charged with enforcing the law. Thus, the vague law prohibits whatever a police officer says it does. Vague laws therefore do not provide due process because under the Constitution, legislatures—not the police—are supposed to make the laws.

There are several cases in which courts have found school rules to be unconstitutionally vague. One such rule forbade "conduct inimical to the best interest of the school." Another prohibited the use of language that "upbraids, abuses or insults any member of the instructional staff." Rules against possessing "medicine" in school have also been found to be unconstitutional, as has a rule against "willfully loitering [hanging out] in a school building without a lawful purpose"—although a rule against loitering in a specific location in a specific school building has been upheld. It is easy to see that reasonable people might disagree about precisely what acts these rules forbid.

"RULES MUST HAVE AN EDUCATIONAL PURPOSE"

Can school officials punish students for off-campus behavior?

Most courts have held that school officials cannot punish students for things they have done away from school. The important question is whether the off-campus behavior has any impact on a student's behavior in school. A New Hampshire court made this distinction when it held that a student who had come to school drunk could not be punished by suspension from school until she worked out the psychological problems between herself and her parents. The court stated that while, under certain circumstances, suspension might be appropriate punishment for drunkenness at a school, "it is fundamentally unfair to keep a student out of school indefinitely because of difficulties between the student and her parents, unless those difficulties manifest themselves in a real threat to school discipline." In other words, the school had no business interfering with a student's problems at home, although it did have the right to punish a student for misconduct in school that might be the result of those problems. On the other hand, a court upheld a school rule that prohibited students from attending off-campus parties at which alcohol was served. The court found that the rule furthered the school's legitimate interest in stopping alcohol abuse by students.

A New Jersey court has held that a student may be temporarily suspended for off-campus acts only if those acts give reasonable cause to believe that a student presents a danger to himself, to others, or to school property. Even that action, the court stated, could be taken only after a hearing.

Many states and school districts have statutes or rules limiting authority of schools over out-of-school activities. In California, Florida, and Louisiana, for instance, schools are allowed to control students' behavior only on school grounds, at school-sponsored activities, and during recesses, as well as on the way to and from school and to and from school activities. Therefore, a federal court of appeals in Louisiana said a student could not be suspended for smoking marijuana off campus. Another board of education restricts its rules against weapons and drugs to "school premises" and "any school activity, function or event."

"RULES MUST NOT PUNISH CONSTITUTIONALLY PROTECTED ACTIVITIES"

Can schools punish students for expressing their views off campus?

Courts have consistently overruled schools that have punished students for out-of-school activities protected by the First Amendment. For example, in one case a court held that a student could not be prohibited from handing out an underground newspaper off of school property. In another case, a New York student who criticized his high-school principal on a radio program went to court when he found that a report of his comments had been placed in his school record. The court ordered the school to remove the report and went on to say, "It is almost inconceivable that in this enlightened day and age a professional administrator could permit the entry in the record of a student of an item which is not only irrelevant but also obviously unconstitutional."

"NOTICE OF CONSEQUENCES OF MISBEHAVIOR MUST BE PROVIDED"

Does a school have to tell students what the punishment is for breaking a rule?

Yes. Some courts have held that school rules must not only be very specific about the conduct they prohibit, but also must spell out the punishments for each violation. For instance, an Ohio court held that a school could not refuse to include in the yearbook a picture of a student whose hair length violated the school's grooming guidelines, because the guidelines had failed to specify the possible punishment for violations. A federal court in Michigan told a school district to revise its proposed student-conduct code because it was extremely vague and general as to the punishments that might be imposed. The court ordered that "the range of corrective action be spelled out for each listed infraction."

In most states, it is enough if the school indicates several possible punishments for a particular rule violation. For example, in an Illinois case, a student was expelled under a school rule prohibiting drugs that specified suspension and only mentioned the possibility of expulsion. The court rejected the student's argument that the rule should have identified exactly which offenses would result in suspension and which in expulsion. In another case, school officials were permitted to forbid a student athlete from participating on his school team for the rest of the year in addition to suspending him for possession of marijuana and alcohol, although he had not been notified that the athletic suspension was a possibility.

Must a school always follow its own rules?

Yes. Even if a school is not required to have written rules or if it could have specified a more severe punishment for particular misconduct, once it adopts a particular rule, it must follow it. Therefore, if a school states that one kind of punishment is the most severe that can be imposed for a particular offense, it cannot then impose a more severe punishment. For example, in one case, even though state law permitted schools to expel students for violating school rules, the court said that for two reasons a student could not be expelled from school for possessing marijuana out of school. First, the local district failed to follow its own rule requiring other disciplinary alternatives before expulsion, and second, its rule concerning drugs did not specifically apply to off-campus possession.

"A SCHOOL MUST HAVE POWER TO IMPOSE PUNISHMENT"

Are there limits on a school's power to regulate student behavior?

Yes. Courts sometimes reject school rules as *ultra vires*. That means that the school has made a rule that it does not have the power to make under state law or under the regulations of the school board. In Ohio, for instance, a court held that where a school board specified that a principal should establish rules on clothing and cleanliness, the principal had no power to also make a rule that regulated the length of students' hair. The court reasoned that if the school board had wanted hair length regulated, it would have said so. Likewise, a Kentucky court struck down a school policy of reducing students' grades when they were absent during suspensions. The court found that while the state law permitted suspensions, it said nothing about academic punishments.

Therefore, if your school wants to punish you, you might want to make sure that the punishment is one that is permitted by state law or board of education regulation.

You should also make sure that the person who wants to punish you has the power to do so. In general, the rule is that the more serious the punishment, the higher the authority required to impose it. For instance, in some states either the principal or the superintendent can suspend a student, but only the superintendent has the power to expel. In other states, principals and superintendents can impose short-term suspensions, but only the school board can impose a suspension of over 21 days.

In most states, only a principal, superintendent, or school board can suspend a student, although some states allow a teacher to suspend, usually for a shorter period of time. If someone other than the principal suspends you, you should also check the state law or school-district rules. In most states, the suspension is illegal. Sometimes a teacher will just tell you not to come to class, but won't call it a suspension. Whatever it is called, not being allowed to go to class has the effect of a suspension and you should request the same rights.

"THE PUNISHMENT MUST BE REASONABLE IN RELATION TO OFFENSE"

What punishments are permitted in school?

The most serious punishments that can be imposed on students are those that deny or limit their right to an education: suspension, expulsion, or suspension from participation in various school activities. These punishments can be imposed only for very serious violations of school rules.

What can a student be suspended for?

The reasons for which students can be suspended from school are usually set out in state law and vary a great deal from state to state. Some state laws simply say that students may be suspended "for good cause." Other states list the specific offenses for which a student may be suspended. Typically, a student may be suspended for offenses involving weapons, drugs, alcohol, or assault.

When a state law sets out the grounds for suspension, you cannot be suspended by a school district for doing something that is not mentioned in the law. For example, if state law says that a student can be suspended only for something that causes a danger of physical injury to others, then a student cannot be suspended simply for disobeying a rule or using bad language. School districts have the power to put even more limits on suspensions. Under New York state law, for example, a student can be suspended who is "insubordinate or disorderly or whose conduct otherwise endangers the safety, morals, health or welfare of others." New York City, however, has chosen to permit suspensions for many fewer reasons.

Some states require schools to try other punishments before imposing a suspension, unless the student's behavior is dangerous or seriously disruptive. In some places, suspensions for truancy are specifically forbidden. Some courts have recognized that suspensions are an extreme measure that undermines the basic aim of a school system—namely, to educate its students. When a student is suspended from school, he or she is, of course, not being educated. Therefore, these courts have said that suspensions should be used only as a last resort and only in an emergency, when there is no other alternative. One court has even said that suspension should be used only to remove unruly students at a particularly tense time. Under this court's reasoning, suspensions should last only as long as the emergency does.

If you want to know the precise legal grounds for suspension in your school, you should look in your state's education law and the bylaws of your school board. Your principal, the school superintendent, or a school-board member can probably tell you where to find these laws.

Can students be suspended because of their parents' behavior?

No. Sometimes schools try to get a student's parents to come to school to discuss their child's work or attitude toward school. When the parents fail to show up, the school may suspend the student or tell her or him not to return until the parents come in. This is illegal. A student can be suspended only for behavior for which the law prescribes suspension. No state makes a parent's unwillingness to come to school grounds for suspending the child. This is because punishing a person for the misconduct of another person violates the right under the Due Process Clause to be free of punishment in the absence of personal guilt.

Students also cannot be suspended just because their parents refuse to comply with other requests of school officials. One court, for example, held that a disabled child could not be suspended because her mother refused to come to school to help take care of her. Likewise, students cannot be suspended or denied access to basic education because of their parents' failure or inability to pay textbook fees.

Finally, even outright misconduct by a parent cannot justify punishing a student. For example, one court has ruled that it was a denial of due process to suspend a student and transfer her to another class because her mother hit her teacher.

What can a student be expelled for?

Expulsion from school means being barred permanently from attending, as opposed to suspension, which means being barred only for a period of time. Permanent expulsion from school may well be illegal in almost all states, in view of the right to an education guaranteed by most states' constitutions. An Alabama court, however, ruled that a student's suspension for nearly a full school year for bringing alcohol to school did not violate the state's compulsory-education law.

Generally, the power to expel students, if it exists at all, is found in state law. The law will usually say who has the power to expel. In some states, only the school board has that power. Many states do not permit school officials to expel students at all. Generally, too, states restrict expulsion to specific offenses. In Texas, for instance, the only ground for expulsion as the first disciplinary action is assault. Students who are found to be "incorrigible"—which means that their behavior cannot be corrected—can be transferred to alternative schools. If they continue to be incorrigible, they can be expelled. In California, a student can be expelled for causing a serious physical injury to another person except in self-defense, for possession of a weapon without a lawful use, for unlawful sale of controlled substances other than small quantities of marijuana, and for robbery or extortion.

Can students be expelled or suspended for committing criminal acts?

Yes. If you are convicted of a crime, including one committed off campus, in most places you can be expelled or at least suspended from school. A federal court in Texas, for example, upheld a school policy of expelling a student for the rest of the school year for "using, selling or possessing a dangerous drug [including marijuana]." The law in many states provides for the suspension or expulsion of a student found to have used or sold narcotics or hallucinogens either on or off campus. In some places, the law requires that a student who has been convicted of a felony (a serious crime, as opposed to a misdemeanor) *must* be expelled.

Can students be suspended if they have been charged with a crime but not yet convicted?

This is a complicated question. One of the most basic concepts of American justice is that a person is considered innocent until proven guilty. Punishment by suspension from school before proof of guilt violates that basic concept. Therefore, the commissioners of education in New York and New Jersey have ruled that a suspension on the basis of an arrest alone is illegal.

Sometimes schools try to get around this problem by holding a suspension hearing to try to prove, before a court trial, that a student committed the offense for which he or she was arrested. If the offense is one related to school activities, the student probably can be suspended even before a court trial. For example, under a Florida statute, a student arrested for a serious crime can be suspended until the case is resolved if the incident "is shown to have an adverse impact on the education program, discipline or welfare of the school in which the student is enrolled." Likewise, a Tennessee court ruled that students can be suspended when juvenile-court charges are pending against them, if it is established at a hearing that "the juvenile poses a danger to persons or property in the school or poses an ongoing threat of disrupting the academic process."

The trouble with having a suspension hearing before your court trial is that anything you say at the hearing may be used against you at trial. Therefore, you should definitely consult a lawyer before attending any school hearing before your trial.

Do students have a right to procedural due process—that is, fair procedures before they can be punished?

Yes. The Supreme Court held in *Goss v. Lopez* that a "student's legitimate entitlement to a public education [is] a property interest which is protected by the Due Process Clause and . . . may not be taken away for misconduct without adherence to the minimum procedures required by that Clause." This means that your right to a free public education is like a piece of property that you own. Just as government officials could not send you to prison or make you pay a heavy fine without following a fair procedure to make sure you really are guilty of a crime, so school officials may not punish you by taking away your right to go to school without following a fair procedure. This makes a lot of sense if you think of the consequences of being deprived of an education on which your ability to go to college or to obtain a good job will depend.

The Supreme Court in *Goss* went on to say that "the Due Process Clause also forbids arbitrary deprivations of liberty. Where a person's good name, reputation, honor or integrity is at stake because of what the government is doing to him, the minimal requirements of the Clause must be satisfied." This means that being found guilty of serious misconduct at school also damages your reputation. The government cannot do this to you without following fair procedures that will insure that you have in fact done what you were accused of.

Although the *Goss* case is extremely important because it

establishes that a student may not be deprived of an education without due process, it does not answer the question of exactly "what process is due"—in other words, what procedures are required in a particular situation. Generally, how much due process is required depends on the seriousness of the charges against a person. For example, no one has a right to as much due process before being made to pay a traffic ticket as they do before they can be sent to prison for robbing a bank. This is true both because the consequences of a conviction for bank robbery are more serious than they are for traffic offenses—a long prison sentence as opposed to a small fine—and because a person's reputation is more seriously damaged by being called a bank robber than an illegal parker. Therefore, it is more important in the serious case to be absolutely sure that the person is guilty. In the context of school discipline, this means that you have a right to little or no due process if the only punishment you face is being forbidden to go to recess, while you have a right to a lot of due process before you can be suspended from school.

Keep in mind that when we speak of a right to due process, we are speaking only of what the law requires school officials to do. Your school may have rules that give you more due-process rights than are required by law.

Can students be punished by being forbidden to participate in extracurricular activities without a hearing?

No. There are punishments other than suspension or expulsion that courts have also found are serious enough to require some due process. One such punishment that schools frequently impose is forbidding a student to participate in extracurricular activities. Courts have recognized that extracurricular activities are generally a fundamental part of the school's educational program. To be denied the opportunity to participate in these activities can be almost as serious a loss of the right to an education as a suspension is. School officials know that, for some students, prohibiting them from playing on a team or going on a class trip would be a more severe punishment than suspending them from school.

A Texas court, for example, concluded that a student was entitled to *more* due process before being dismissed from an honor society and from a student group organized to foster school spirit, than before being suspended for one day. Membership in both groups required several years of diligent effort. Therefore, the court held, before the school could forbid the student from participating, she was entitled to a hearing. On the other hand, another court held that a student was entitled to no more due process when his punishment was a full-year athletic suspension as well as a short suspension from school, than he would have a right to if the suspension from school were the only punishment.

In an Arkansas case, a federal court ruled that a student could not be suspended from a football team without notice of the charge against him and a chance to present his side of the story. The court found that the student had an important interest in participation in interscholastic sports, particularly since he was a senior applying for college athletic scholarships. A New York court held that a student who was charged with drinking a glass of beer in violation of the school's code of conduct for members of athletic teams could not be deprived of his varsity letters without a hearing.

The New York State Commissioner of Education has explained why school officials must act fairly when excluding students from extracurricular activities. In ruling that a school could not prevent students from running for office where it had no evidence that they were responsible for obscene posters, he wrote:

> *Full participation in extra-curricular activities may not be restricted on the basis of fiat: to justify such action, there must be a legal basis for curtailment—and, in addition, the extent of disciplinary exclusion must be neither arbitrary, capricious nor unreasonable. . . . Basic fairness dictates that the student and the person in parental relation to him be given an opportunity to appear informally before the administrator authorized to impose discipline and to discuss the factual situation underlying the threatened disciplinary action.*

Do students have a right to due process before being excluded from transportation to school?

Exclusion from transportation to school is another punishment requiring due process. If you have no other way to get to school besides the school bus, exclusion from the bus is as serious a punishment as suspension or expulsion. One court ruled, however, that a student could be kicked off the bus first and given a hearing afterward.

May students be excluded from lunch for disciplinary reasons?

Exclusion from lunch may also be impermissible. If students are eligible for free or reduced-price meals at school, it is a violation of the National School Lunch Act to discipline them by restricting their access to meals served at school. Even if you do not receive these meals, you should never be prevented from eating lunch somewhere, since such a punishment would have no educational purpose and could be bad for your health.

Do students have a right to due process before being transferred to another school?

In many states, students have a right to a hearing before being transferred to another school for disciplinary reasons. In New York, for example, before a principal even requests a transfer, students are entitled to an informal conference. They are also entitled to have the reasons for the transfer request put in writing. Then, students have a right to a formal due-process hearing before the superintendent where they may be represented by a lawyer and may present witnesses. A record must be kept of the hearing.

In Texas, before students can be transferred to an alternative-education program for "incorrigible students," they have a right to a hearing at which it must be shown either that the student presents a clear and present danger of physical harm to himself or herself or to others, or that the student engages in serious or persistent misbehavior in violation of published standards of student conduct and that "all reasonable alternatives to the pupil's regular classroom program, including a variety of discipline management techniques have been exhausted."

Several courts have ruled that because transfers involve serious consequences for students, they have the right to notice and to due-process hearings similar to those required for expulsion. As one court put it, "To transfer a pupil during a school year would be a terrifying experience for many children of normal sensibilities. . . . Realistically, I think many, if not most students would consider a short suspension a less drastic form of punishment than an involuntary transfer, especially if the transferee school was farther from home or had poorer physical or educational facilities."

In one case where a student was transferred to a night-school program, a court ordered a formal hearing with an impartial hearing officer who was not an administrator from the student's school. The court observed, "Considering the Board's transfer policy and the fundamental differences between a GED certificate and a standard diploma, this amounts to the functional equivalent of an absolute expulsion."

If you are threatened with a transfer to another school, make sure that the person threatening to transfer you has the power to do so. In many school districts, only the superintendent of schools, not the principal, has the power to transfer students.

May students be barred from attending graduation for disciplinary reasons without a hearing?

No. Some courts have held that school officials may not discipline students by barring them from graduation exercises. In a 1971 case in New York, the court ruled that a school district could not bar a high-school student who had satisfactorily completed her studies but who had allegedly struck and threatened her principal during a disturbance at the school. The court ruled there was no evidence that her presence at graduation ceremonies would be disruptive, so that barring her from participating would not be "a reasonable punishment meant to encourage the best educational results." It added: "It would indeed be a distortion of our educational process in this period of youthful discontent to snatch from a young woman at the point of educational fruition the savoring of her educational success."

Similarly, the decision of a New York City junior high school to bar a student from graduation exercises was reversed by the New York State Commissioner of Education because the grounds for her punishment—"lack of good citizenship"—were too vague. In addition, the commissioner said: "It is educationally unsound for a school system to brand an individual with the label of 'poor citizen.' The placing of such a label upon a student is not a proper function of a school system."

When a married, pregnant student was barred from graduation exercises because of her condition, the New York State

Commissioner of Education again overruled the school district's decision.

In another case, however, school officials upheld the action of school officials in barring a student from graduation because he had failed to turn in on time required paperwork proving that he had completed an independent study assignment.

Students have a substantial interest in receiving a diploma and therefore it cannot be denied without due process. For instance, in one case in which the student was denied permission to take certain state-administered exams after being accused of cheating, and as a result did not receive an official diploma, the court found she was entitled to a hearing to determine whether she was in fact guilty of the charges.

Some courts have found that students have a legally recognized interest in participating in graduation ceremonies, and thus that due process is required before a student is barred. But one court has said that while students have an interest in their diploma they do not have a protected interest in the graduation ceremony itself; therefore, it found no due-process requirement.

Can students' grades be lowered for disciplinary reasons?

School policies vary widely from state to state about whether a student's grade may be lowered as punishment for absences. In New York, the education commissioner has ruled that cutting class and truancy are behavioral, not academic, offenses. While students can receive disciplinary sanctions for unexcused absences, they should not receive automatic grade reductions or failures. For this reason, one court has recently held that a school rule requiring teachers to lower students' grades 4 percent each day they are suspended from school was unlawful.

If class participation is part of the grade, that policy should be announced at the beginning of the term, and absent students should have an opportunity to make up missed work regardless of whether their absence was excused or not.

In another state there are regulations forbidding the lowering of grades but permitting school boards to set attendance policies that deny students credit altogether. The rationale is that the averaging in of a low or failing grade will have a permanent punitive effect on the student's record, while simply denying credit allows the student to make up the class by starting over fresh. Students must be given adequate notice of such attendance policies; then, if necessary, an opportunity for a hearing; and, if the absence is legitimate, a chance to make up missed work. If a student is prone to cutting or truancy, he or she must have counseling.

In some states, school districts have been found to be exceeding their authority in setting policies providing for automatic grade reductions or loss of credit after a certain number of absences; such rules are not included in or permitted by state statutes dealing with truancy.

In one case, a college student who was removed from a program challenged the college's policy that said that students who miss four classes "may" be so removed. The court ruled that the decision was arbitrary because the school did not attempt to evaluate the effect of absences and should have given the student a chance to show that he had learned the material covered in his absence.

In another case, a school reduced a student's grade in several courses after she left school for an emergency, without advising the school staff as was required by the school policy on unexcused absences. The court said the school had to show that the grade-reduction penalty in this girl's case was reasonably related to the disciplinary objectives of the school board's policy on unexcused absences.

Some states and many school districts have laws or rules requiring schools to permit suspended students to make up work and take final exams. A Kentucky court ruled that a school that said in its handbook that suspended students were subject to grade reductions for days missed and could not make up missed work, exceeded its authority in imposing this extra penalty because the state law on suspensions did not provide for academic penalties. The New York State Commissioner of Education has ruled that school boards "may not subvert the purpose of grading by arbitrarily reducing a student's grades as a means of imposing discipline." The New Jersey State Commissioner of Education has prohibited schools from counting student absences during suspensions to determine breaches by students of attendance policy, because that would constitute a forbidden double penalty. A suspended student must be given the opportunity to make up any work missed and must be graded as if the work had been received on time.

What due process is required before a student can be suspended from school?

In *Goss v. Lopez*, the United States Supreme Court recognized that suspending a student from school deprives that person of education and reputation, and went on to discuss exactly what procedures must be followed before a student may be suspended. The case before the Court involved a ten-day suspension, and thus the opinion dealt only with the minimum due-process rights required for short suspensions, suggesting that where longer suspensions are involved, students are entitled to additional due-process guarantees. In any event, the Court held that before a student may be suspended for any length of time, he or she must be given oral or written notice of the charges. If the student denies the charges, the school must provide an explanation of the evidence the authorities have, and the student must be given an opportunity to present her or his side of the story. The Court held further that, except in emergency situations, the notice of charges and hearing should precede a student's suspension, and where this is not possible because a student poses a danger to persons or property or an ongoing threat of disruption, the notice and hearing "should follow as soon as practicable."

The Supreme Court noted that longer suspensions or expulsions "may require more formal procedures." In fact, many states have passed statutes providing extensive due-process protections for both short- and long-term suspensions. Connecticut's law, for example, provides for informal and formal hearings for suspensions of varying lengths and for expulsion, setting time limits on suspensions and expulsion. It also provides that suspended students be permitted to complete any classwork and examinations missed during the suspension and that some form of alternative education be arranged for expelled students.

Do students have the right to notice of charges before they can be punished?

Yes. Before you can be severely punished, you have a right to know exactly what the school says you have done wrong. A hearing is useless if you have no idea what accusations you are supposed to be defending yourself against. The idea is one of the oldest in criminal law and is now also established in such administrative proceedings as school suspension hearings.

Often a student is charged with "violating school rules" or "serious misconduct"—phrases that fail to give any idea of what offense has been committed or what rule has been violated. That is not adequate notice. A federal court in Washington,

D.C., has required that the notice state "specific, clear and full reasons for the proposed action, including the specification of the alleged act upon which the disciplinary action is to be based and the reference to the regulation subsection under which such action is proposed." In addition, some courts have required that, for longer suspensions, the student be provided with a short summary of the evidence of wrongdoing.

In a 1974 case, a Wisconsin federal court held that a letter given to a student's parents stating that "your son . . . continues to conduct himself in an irresponsible and disruptive manner" and "has been deliberately defiant of reasonable requests by teachers . . . on three occasions within the past few weeks" did not satisfy due-process requirements of adequate notice of the charges. The court found that the lack of specificity of the charges adversely affected the student's ability to prepare a defense and thus the meaningfulness of the opportunity to be heard.

Sometimes misconduct is so obvious that courts have not required the school to give much notice of the charges. In one such case, students got into a fight, injured a school administrator who tried to break it up, and damaged her office.

In addition, courts have held that students have a right to know the charges sufficiently in advance of the hearing to permit them "to examine the charges, prepare a defense and gather evidence and witnesses." The Supreme Court in *Goss* held that the notice given to a student in a case involving the possibility of a short suspension could be either oral or in writing. For longer suspensions, other courts have held that notice must be in writing.

In some states, statutes or regulations require schools to provide specific information about charges to students and their parents. One state, for instance, requires advance written notice of charges that includes mention of the proposed punishment and the student's procedural rights. In another state, before a superintendent can suspend a student, the law requires written notice that includes a list of the school's potential witnesses, the possible consequences of the hearing, the student's due-process rights, a list of free or low-cost legal services, and, of course, the specific charges.

A student suspension cannot be based on charges other than those specified to the student in advance of the hearing. In other words, schools cannot charge students with one offense and then find them guilty of another, because, in the words of one judge, to do so would "render meaningless the opportunity to present their side of the case."

Do students have the right to an impartial hearing officer?

Yes. For serious punishments you have the right to have your hearing held before someone who was not involved in the incident and is not prejudiced against you. This will usually be a member of the school board, but sometimes even board members are too involved to be fair judges of your case, and you should ask for someone who is.

In some states, statutes or regulations specify who may serve as hearing officers. In California, for instance, a hearing panel must consist of three or more school-district employees who are not members of the staff of the accused student's school. In Washington, D.C., schools, one court mandated "independent hearing officers" unconnected with the school system for suspensions of over two days. In contrast, the California Supreme Court found nothing wrong with teachers serving as hearing officers.

When hearing officers have had prior involvement in the incidents which led to suspension, a number of courts have overturned the suspensions. For instance, when a Texas student was arrested in 1972 on a drug charge and the school board discussed the matter with law-enforcement officials before suspending him, a federal court ruled that the student was entitled to a hearing before the state commissioner of education.

The New York State Commissioner of Education has said that a hearing cannot be held before a school superintendent who has been involved at an earlier stage of the case. Similarly, a court in Michigan held in 1972 that where serious punishment such as transfer was intended, a principal who witnessed the incident leading up to the charges could not hear the case. In another case, a court found an expulsion hearing to be unfair because the school district's attorneys acted both as prosecutors and as legal advisors to the board that heard the case. Moreover, the superintendent who was involved in the prosecution sat in with the board during its deliberations.

In a Texas case in 1981, however, a court refused to find a violation when the school-board attorney acted as both prosecutor against the student and advisor to the board. And one court has ruled that a school official is not automatically disqualified from serving on a hearing panel because of prior involvement as an investigator and a witness against the student, unless "his involvement in an incident created a bias such as to preclude his affording the student an impartial hearing."

The hearing officer's decision must be made solely on the evidence presented at the hearing, not on privately obtained information. In one case, the New York Commissioner of Education said the decision as to whether the student was guilty could not be based solely on the superintendent's personal knowledge of the student's arrest for alleged drug possession. He wrote,

> *It is impossible for the student to cross-examine or in any way rebut the private, nontestimonial knowledge of the hearing officer. . . . [P]erhaps most serious, is*

> the fact that the hearing officer loses his neutral pos-
> ture and, in effect, becomes a salient witness in sup-
> port of the charges.

To establish whether the person or board hearing your case
may have prejudged it, you should ask for the right to question
them about their previous knowledge of the incidents at issue.

Do students have the right to demand an open or closed hearing?

Sometimes students want to have a private disciplinary hearing
so that no one knows that they have been accused of doing
something wrong. Other times, students may want people to
come to the hearing to make sure that school officials act fairly.
The general rule is that a student disciplinary hearing, unlike a
court trial, will be closed to the public unless the student, parent, or guardian requests that it be open. The federal law governing privacy of student records can be used to protect the
confidentiality of the proceedings. This law prohibits release of
student records, either orally or in writing, without written
parental consent. You also have the right to exclude from the
hearing anyone without a legitimate interest in it. Some courts
have also said that you have the right to insist that the hearing
be open to the public. However, other courts have ruled that
school authorities have the right to keep the public out, even
against your wishes.

Do students have the right to a lawyer at a school disciplinary hearing?

Yes. Courts have held that students have the right to a lawyer
where serious consequences, such as long-term suspension or
expulsion, might result from a hearing. But in *Goss v. Lopez*,
the Supreme Court explicitly refused to require that students

be permitted to be represented by counsel at school disciplinary hearings involving short suspensions—ten days or less. The Court made clear, however, that longer suspensions or expulsions might require more formal proceedings, including the right to counsel, and even suggested that in "difficult cases," school officials might permit counsel even though only a short suspension was involved.

Some states specify in statutes that students have the right to a lawyer at school disciplinary hearings. Some student discipline codes inform students that they have the right to a lawyer before long-term suspension or expulsion may be imposed. In one state, the student can choose a representative to be present for a hearing on short-term suspensions, but the representative cannot act as a lawyer for the student unless the school district also has a lawyer present. In contrast, before an expulsion hearing, the student must receive notice of the right to be represented by counsel.

Another example of consequences serious enough to warrant the right to a lawyer appears in a New York case. There the court ruled that a student had a right to a lawyer when, as a result of being accused of cheating on an examination, she was denied credit for the exam and was prohibited from taking other exams.

No court has ruled that low-income students must be provided with a lawyer free of charge, but some courts have required school districts to provide lists of free or low-cost legal services. If you are threatened with serious punishment and cannot afford a lawyer, you should ask to be given one— even if it is unlikely the school district will do so. In case you later want to go to court, you can show that you did ask.

Do students have the right to remain silent at a school disciplinary hearing?

Yes. The right to remain silent, that is, not to be required to testify against yourself, is guaranteed by the Fifth Amendment to the Constitution. You will rarely have occasion to claim this right, however, as you will almost always want to tell your side of the story. The most likely situation in which you might want to remain silent is when you have had criminal charges brought against you for the same conduct that led to the suspension, or if you think criminal charges might be brought. If the suspension hearing is held before the criminal trial, you may want to remain silent because what you say about your conduct could be used against you in the criminal trial. Under these circumstances, a federal court has held that "one cannot be denied his Fifth Amendment right to remain silent merely because he is a student." That means your refusal to testify at a disciplinary hearing cannot be used against you as an admission of guilt.

You should make such a decision only after you talk to a lawyer. If you and your lawyer think it is important for you to remain silent because of criminal charges, you might ask that the hearing be postponed until after the criminal trial and that you be allowed to attend classes until the hearing.

Do students have the right to bring witnesses to a disciplinary hearing?

The Supreme Court held in *Goss v. Lopez* that schools are not required to let students bring witnesses to a hearing involving suspensions of less than ten days. Other courts have held that you have such a right, at least for longer suspensions.

The chancellor of the New York City school system held that it was illegal for school officials to deny a student the right to produce a teacher to testify on his behalf by refusing to release the teacher from his duties or pay him for the time he spent at the hearing, since school officials were given time to testify against the student.

**Do students have the right to question their accusers
at a school disciplinary hearing?**

The right to know the identity of the person who has accused
you of wrongdoing and to cross-examine (question) that person is very important in criminal law. This right "to confront
your accusers" at trial is guaranteed by the Sixth Amendment
to the Constitution. The Supreme Court has also said that the
right is required at welfare hearings. The right has been held to
be equally applicable to school suspensions and other administrative hearings. It is understandable that the accusers may be
afraid of retaliation by the person they accuse. This may be a
real problem, but the people who wrote the Constitution were
even more concerned about the possibility of false charges
against innocent persons by anonymous accusers motivated
by personal feelings of malice or prejudice.

Nevertheless, school principals sometimes suspend students
on the basis of complaints from teachers or other students, but
refuse to give out the names of these complainants. This problem is illustrated by a 1971 New Jersey case involving two girls
who had been assaulted by other students. Witnesses to the incident identified the attackers, but requested that their names not
be revealed because they were afraid of being beaten up themselves. At the hearing, the accused students claimed they were
innocent, but they were not permitted to question their
accusers. Their case went to the New Jersey Supreme Court,
which ruled that the students had a right to question their
accusers. The witnesses' fears, the court said, were no basis for
denying the accused students their constitutional rights.

Although the Supreme Court in *Goss v. Lopez* refused to
require schools to provide for confrontation and cross-examination of witnesses in connection with short suspensions, it
again stated that in "unusual circumstances" it might be advis-
able to allow a student to cross-examine opposing witnesses.

97

Most courts in recent years have held that the circumstances of a long-term suspension justify providing the right of cross-examination. In addition, the right is guaranteed by statute in some states.

A Pennsylvania court held that the requirement of a "proper hearing" for student suspensions meant the student must have an "opportunity to face accusers, hear their testimony, and examine all witnesses testifying against him." In 1982, a California court said that a student could not be suspended for fighting because the facts surrounding the incident were hotly disputed and no witnesses testified at the hearing. Written statements from witnesses were not enough.

You should always request the opportunity to confront your accusers. Some courts have ruled that you must be given the names of witnesses whom the school will produce to testify against you, as well as a report on the facts they will testify about. The New Jersey State Commissioner of Education has required that students be given any witnesses' statements before the hearing. Some school districts go beyond the courts' basic requirements, and permit students to question their accusers even at informal short-term suspension conferences. In one school district, for instance, a suspension cannot go on a student's permanent record unless he or she is afforded that right.

In some recent cases, however, courts have held that the accusers' identities do not have to be revealed at a school disciplinary hearing. These courts have reasoned that school officials are generally acquainted with student accusers, have access to their disciplinary records, and can discover easily if the accusers and the accused have been friends in the past or whether the accuser may have a motive for making a false accusation. Since this is the kind of information that would be revealed by questioning the accuser, cross-examination would simply duplicate the information the administrator already knows. The courts therefore found that the burden on the school of permitting cross-examination would be greater than the benefits of doing so.

For similar reasons, other courts have also upheld the decision of school officials not to require a coach and a teacher to be present for questioning by students whom they had accused of misconduct. The hearing officer cannot, however, automatically give more weight to the school's evidence than to the student's testimony. For instance, one court overturned a suspension where a dean said he had, on principle, accepted a security officer's version of an incident over the student's. The court noted, "While this 'principle' has currency in many totalitarian countries, the court is not aware of its existence as a principle of Anglo-Saxon law."

In places where students do not have the right to confront their accusers, the school can use hearsay evidence—that is, written statements or testimony by one person about what another person said to him or her concerning the incident. In most places, however, a suspension cannot be based on hearsay alone. California law, for instance, states that hearsay alone is inadequate for an expulsion.

Whatever the law in your school district about your right to know the identity of your accusers and to question them, you should always request the opportunity to do so. If you have been falsely accused by someone, questioning that person may be the only way you can establish your innocence. By making them tell more than what is in their written statements or by bringing out inconsistencies in the testimony against you, you may be able to convince school officials that you are innocent or at least to show that you had an excuse for what you did.

Who has the burden of proof at a school disciplinary hearing? In other words, must you prove you are innocent, or must the school prove you are guilty?

Your school or school district bears the burden of proving that you did what they say you did and also that its disciplinary response is appropriate. In the words of one state education commissioner:

> *Before a pupil may be disciplined, whether it be by expulsion, suspension or curtailment of privileges, two essential elements must be present. There must be some conduct which serves as the predicate for the imposition of discipline and there must be a reasonable degree of certainty that the pupil was the perpetrator of, or otherwise participated in such conduct.*
>
> *It is clear that the responsibility for establishing both elements in a disciplinary situation rests with the school officials. It is equally well settled that the student must be afforded the basic presumption of innocence of wrongdoing until his guilt has been established by direct, competent evidence of misconduct.*

The burden on the school to prove a student's guilt is not as great as it would be in a criminal court, where guilt has to be proven "beyond a reasonable doubt." For example, a school was allowed to expel a student simply because he had said that cigarettes in his possession contained marijuana, according to a Michigan court. A series of Florida cases involving the sale of caffeine pills illustrates the different sorts of evidence required to prove wrongdoing. The court said the school could expel students who said they had been buying or selling "speed," the street name for amphetamines, an illegal substance, even though the pills were actually caffeine and were neither controlled nor illegal. The students' statements to school officials showed they thought they were dealing in drugs; thus, their statements were adequate grounds for expulsion. But the court argued that a third student could not be expelled, even though she too had been selling caffeine pills, because there was no evidence she had pretended to her customers that they were "speed."

Courts are reluctant to second-guess school districts when it comes to student discipline. Generally, they will overturn a suspension only if there is clearly *no* evidence offered of wrongdoing or if the school district's action is entirely arbitrary. A court might rehear all the evidence and draw its own conclusion if the school district has not kept a record of the original hearing, but it is unlikely to overturn a suspension or expulsion simply because it is excessive punishment. This is true even when the court finds the punishment harsh. This happened in a 1985 Mississippi case where the students were expelled for a single act of graffiti (painting the number "I" on a school wall). The court disapproved of the punishment and urged the school system not to impose it, but said, "Dissatisfactions with such rules must be addressed to the school board, not the courts of this state."

Do students have the right to a record of a school disciplinary hearing?

It would be difficult, if not impossible, to challenge the outcome of a disciplinary hearing without a complete record of what went on at the hearing. For this reason, a number of courts have required schools to maintain a complete record and make it available to the student on request. Generally, a tape recording is all that is required, but some courts have said that schools must make a written transcript of the tape and provide it to the student on request. Other courts have said that a student has a right

101

to make a recording of the hearing. Some states require schools to maintain word-for-word records. But as a general rule, this requirement pertains only in cases involving longer suspensions or expulsions.

Do students have the right to written findings after a school disciplinary hearing?

Maybe. To appeal a suspension, it is important to have the findings, that is, a written decision that discusses the testimony and states the reason for imposing the suspension; otherwise, the person reviewing the case on appeal cannot determine whether there was a legal basis for the suspension.

Most—but not all—courts that have dealt with this issue have agreed that students are entitled to a written statement of the facts that support the hearing officer's decision. Written findings may also be required by your state's statutes or regulations.

As a result of a 1985 case in New York City, hearing officers must notify students of their decision by telephone or mailgram within two days of the hearing and must mail out a written decision within five days. This written decision must explain the reasons for the determination, indicate the relevant evidence, and include factual findings as well as specify where and when the student can return to school. The decision must be implemented within five days of the hearing.

Do students have the right to appeal an adverse decision?

Most school districts permit an appeal after the suspension or expulsion hearing, and many states spell out appeal procedures in their statutes concerning student discipline. Typically, an appeal goes to the superintendent and then to the school board. In some states, students have the right to a further appeal to the state commissioner or state board of education. The letter advising you of your suspension should provide information on how to appeal. If it does not, you should ask (in writing) your school-board office or state department of education. You can appeal based on the school's failure to follow proper procedures, the lack of evidence, the excessiveness of the punishment, the unfairness of the rule, or anything else that is unfair or in violation of established policy. You should refer to the record of the hearing and to the hearing officer's written findings if they exist. (If no record or findings exist, that in itself is a ground for appeal.) You can ask to be returned to school, to be transferred to another school, to have the suspension removed from your record, etc. At this stage a lawyer is important.

Although some courts have guaranteed the right to appeal, appeals after hearings are not always required. If your school district or state has no appeal procedures, you may have to go to court to challenge your suspension.

Do students lose the right to an education during a long-term suspension?

No. Some states require schools to provide alternative instruction to students of compulsory-attendance age. The New York State Commissioner of Education has ruled that this instruction must be adequate to enable the student to complete all of her or his coursework. If, for instance, the student was taking a computer class, a computer must be available. If the student was enrolled in a Spanish class, a Spanish tutor must be provided. The New Jersey State Commissioner of Education has ruled that a suspended student must have the opportunity to make up missed work . In one New York case, a judge said that even though the student was suspended for only five days, giving him homework assignments was not enough. The school should have also provided tutoring.

In some school districts, students may be transferred to an

alternative-education site instead of being expelled. These in-school suspensions are increasingly used as an alternative short-term suspension. Some states question the practice. For instance, as the Kentucky Department of Education notes in its *Student Discipline Guidelines*, this is "a common practice among schools seeking to avoid the complications of actual suspension" and is unacceptable unless the student is placed in a program that provides close supervision and structured study. A Kentucky Attorney General's opinion concludes, "'In-school suspension' is a contradiction in terms and not within the disciplinary procedures authorized by statute, and if an 'in-school suspended' child is not being afforded an alternative educational program and school counseling, the child is legally absent from school." Whether or not they offer alternative instruction, in-school suspensions remove students from their regular classrooms and should therefore entitle them to the same due-process protections as out-of-school suspensions of the same duration.

Do students who are above the age of compulsory school have a right to due process?

Yes. The right to go to school lasts longer than the obligation. While you may not be compelled to attend school past the age of sixteen or seventeen, you usually have a right to attend until you are twenty-one (check your state's law for the exact age). Students above the compulsory attendance age have the same due-process rights as younger students.

What should students do if they believe school discipline is administered in a racially discriminatory manner?

Federal Office of Civil Rights statistics have shown that minority students are suspended at dramatically higher rates than are white students. In a landmark case in 1974, a federal court found that racial disparities in disciplinary action in Dallas came from illegal discrimination and did not simply reflect more misbehavior by minority students. The court said several factors contributed to the disparity, including: (1) the tendency of school staff to refer minority students for discipline more frequently and punish them more harshly than whites for equivalent conduct; (2) punishment for cultural differences such as wearing hats or different styles of personal conduct; and (3) provocation of minority students as a result of "insensitivity," "personal racism," and the very existence of a "white-controlled institution." In a similar challenge in Newburgh, New York, a school district agreed to a timetable of eliminating racial disparity in its suspension rates. The district consented to set up committees composed of teachers, students, parents, community representatives, and the principal from each school. These committees would consider proposals to change and clarify the discipline code, to provide assistance to teachers with high discipline-referral rates, and to tutor students whose behavior problems were related to low achievement. The school district also said it would increase the percentage of minority teachers and train all school staff in discipline and race relations.

In another case, an Arkansas court found that school rules were vague and allowed for too much discretion by teachers. This resulted in black students being disciplined for certain behavior for which white students were not. The court ordered that "uniform and objective guidelines be established to eliminate the opportunity to administer discipline on an uneven-handed basis." Courts have considered disciplinary practices in the course of designing remedies for unconstitutional segregation of schools. For instance, in a Benton Harbor, Michigan, desegregation case in 1981, the court ordered that a biracial committee develop a uniform discipline code to include an appeal procedure to a biracial panel in the case of suspension or expulsion. The court also stated that the "use of suspension or expulsion should be limited to a last resort and the committee should explore the use of effective alternatives to suspension or expulsion."

If you believe that your school is guilty of racially discriminatory practices or of excessive use of suspensions and expulsions, you should seek the help of local civil-rights or student-advocacy groups to convince the school to adopt more evenhanded and educationally sound practices. You can obtain recent suspension data on your school district from the National Coalition of Advocates for Students in Boston. You can also file a freedom of information request with your school district, which may (and should) collect data on the rate of suspensions for specific offenses among various ethnic and racial groups. In New York City, this data revealed that minority students were suspended more frequently than other students for smoking, truancy, lateness, and poor academic achievement. The Board of Education eventually signed an agreement with the Office of Civil Rights not to suspend anyone for these offenses.

8

CORPORAL PUNISHMENT

Is corporal punishment legal?

Regrettably, it may be. Corporal punishment means physical punishment such as spanking or paddling. In 1977, the Supreme Court held in *Ingraham v. Wright*[1] that "moderate" corporal punishment does not violate the constitutional prohibition against cruel and unusual punishments contained in the Eighth Amendment, or the guarantee of liberty contained in the Fourteenth Amendment. This means that a public school system may, within limits, permit teachers or other school officials to hit students without violating the Constitution.

The *Ingraham* decision is shocking because it means that the public schools are the *only* government-run institutions where corporal punishment is allowed. Corporal punishment has been prohibited for many years in the military services and, more recently, in prisons and mental hospitals as well. In a case involving corporal punishment of prisoners in Arkansas, a court held that the use of the strap "offends contemporary concepts of decency and human dignity and precepts of civilization." It does not make much sense that government officials can hit schoolchildren if they cannot hit prisoners. This is particularly true since it is the job of schools to teach students to work out problems without violence. The school does not set a good example if it cannot control students' behavior without hitting them.

Just because a school *may* permit corporal punishment does not mean that it *must* do so. In fact, 25 states* and a large number of municipalities and school districts have laws and regulations that forbid school officials and employees from hitting students. Since many of the states that prohibit corporal punishment are those that have the largest populations, corporal punishment is, in fact, prohibited in more schools than it is permitted.

Many other schools that still permit corporal punishment have rules that limit its use. For example, there may be a rule that students must know ahead of time what behavior can be punished by corporal punishment. Another common rule is that corporal punishment may not be used until some other punishment has been tried first and failed. Some schools have a rule that a school official may not physically punish a student unless there is another adult present. Some schools do not permit the use of any kind of whip or paddle or other object for inflicting corporal punishment. Finally, some schools have rules that students must be given the chance to explain their behavior and why they should not be physically punished

---

* According to the National Center for the Study of Corporal Punishment and Alternatives, the following states prohibit corporal punishment: Alaska, California, Connecticut, Hawaii, Illinois, Iowa, Maine, Maryland, Massachusetts, Michigan, Minnesota, Montana, Nebraska, Nevada, New Hampshire, New Jersey, New York, North Dakota, Oregon, Rhode Island, Utah, Vermont, Virginia, Washington, and Wisconsin.

before the punishment is inflicted on them. Although school officials are not required by the Constitution to have parents' permission to strike a child, some schools require that parents be notified before their child is punished. Some schools permit parents to request ahead of time that their child not be given corporal punishment.

When is corporal punishment excessive?

The Supreme Court has ruled that "excessive" physical punishment of students is illegal in schools. A punishment is considered excessive if it was unnecessary and unreasonable under the circumstances—that is, if it is inflicted for a minor offense like chewing gum—and if it leaves an injury. Students can sue teachers who inflict excessive corporal punishment on them. In order to do this, you would have to be able to show medical reports and photographs of your injuries, and your doctor would have to testify at a trial. Therefore, if you believe that you have been subjected to excessive corporal punishment it is very important to see a doctor so that you will be able to prove it. This should be done with the guidance of a lawyer.

Unfortunately, in most cases in which students have sought to prove that the corporal punishment inflicted on them was excessive, courts have upheld the actions of school officials. This is so even though in many cases severe injuries were inflicted on the students. For example, in *Ingraham* the student was subjected to more than 20 blows with a paddle while being held over a table in the principal's office. He suffered a hematoma (a very bad bruise), which required medical attention and kept him out of school for several days.

What can students do if they are subjected to excessive or unlawful corporal punishment?

Students can press criminal charges for assault against teachers who hurt them or who do not follow school rules for inflicting corporal punishment. A complaint by a student to school authorities about unfair and excessive corporal punishment can also result in a teacher's being disciplined or even fired.

Corporal punishment is unconstitutional if it is inflicted in a racially discriminatory way. Courts in Texas and Louisiana, for example, ruled that teachers who hit students because of racial prejudice can be sued in court. Two courts in Texas also found that minority students received corporal punishment more often than did white students and they ordered the schools to change the way they inflicted corporal punishment.

There is some reason to hope that in the future corporal punishment will be banned in all schools. One of the reasons for the Supreme Court's decision in *Ingraham* was that corporal punishment had traditionally been permitted in public schools and that state law permitting students to sue or press criminal charges against teaches who abused them physically provided enough safeguards against excessive corporal punishment to make the practice constitutional. In the 20 years since the decision in *Ingraham*, the public has become much more aware of the problem of child abuse and no longer approves so readily of hitting children.

The National Education Association, a nationwide organization of teachers, and the American Public Health Association, among other organizations, have opposed the use of corporal punishment in schools. Since corporal punishment is now permitted only in a minority of schools, the Supreme Court's reasoning that it is constitutional because most people approve of it is no longer very persuasive. It is important for students to find out exactly what the rules are about corporal punishment in their own schools. If corporal punishment is permitted in your school, you might want to try to convince your school to prohibit it in the future.

Do schools have the legal obligation to protect students from assaults by other students?

Usually not. There are a number of cases in which students have attempted to sue school officials who failed to protect them against physical assaults by other students. In almost every case, courts have held that the schools were not responsible for protecting the students in these situations. The law concerning sexual harassment by other students is discussed in chapter 3.

9

LAW ENFORCEMENT AND SEARCHES

In a recent case involving school discipline, a federal court pointed to a study that reported that in the 1940s schoolteachers listed talking, chewing gum, and running in the hallways as the primary disciplinary problems they encountered. The court went on to note that today's teachers are more concerned with drug abuse, rape, robbery, assault, burglary, arson, and bombings. As drug use and violent crime in schools have become a major problem, schools have increased the practice of searching students, and the presence of security guards and armed police in the schools is more and more common. While it is certainly important to keep drugs and weapons out of schools to provide a safe environment for learning, students' right to privacy is also very important. Once a school reaches the point where students are being watched by surveillance devices, fingerprinted for identification, eavesdropped on in class by undercover police agents, or confronted in the halls by security guards, the school begins to resemble a prison—and learning becomes difficult, if not impossible, for many.

Finding the right balance between the needs of law enforcement and the privacy rights of students has been a major concern of courts in the last two decades.

Are all police officers allowed to question or arrest students in school?

The Fifth Amendment to the Constitution provides that no person shall be compelled in any criminal case to be a witness against himself. Thus, although school officials may allow the police to come into schools to question or arrest students, neither school officials nor anybody else can make students talk to the police. You have a constitutional right to remain silent. The practice in some schools, however, is for school officials to cooperate with police investigations by taking students from class and making them available for questioning. Other states and local school districts have set limits on this practice. In some places, schools may allow police to conduct investigations in school only if the alleged offense was committed on school property. School officials cannot require students to submit to a police interview in school, and a school official must stay with a student who agrees to be questioned. The principal cannot allow police to remove a student from school unless the student is under arrest. If a student is arrested, a parent or guardian must be notified and a school official must stay with the student until the parent arrives.

The Cleveland, Ohio, schools have provided detailed instructions for principals regarding student interrogation by police:

When law enforcement authorities want to question a student at school, the principal must try to contact the student's parent or guardian to give the authorities permission to do so. The parent or guardian may refuse; request interrogation only in his/her presence;

113

or request that the principal act in the role of the parent during the interrogation.

If the parent or guardian cannot be reached, the principal may deny or allow the questioning.

Whenever the principal acts in the place of the parent or legal guardian, the principal must:

a. *Ensure that the student has been advised of his/her rights.*

b. *Be present during the entire interrogation.*

c. *Not enter into the interrogation on behalf of the authority.*

d. *Interrupt the interrogation to protect the pupil from abusive or threatening questioning.*

e. *End the interrogation when it becomes obvious that a formal charge is likely.*

Many school-district policies and discipline codes require school officials to call in police whenever a crime, including possession of a weapon or drugs, is committed on school grounds.

What should a student do if the police want to question him or her?

If you are interviewed by the police, you have the right to remain silent, and this is usually the best course to take until you have spoken to your parents or a lawyer. You should be polite and give the police your name and address. If they do not know who you are, they may be more likely to arrest you since they may not be able to maintain contact with you any other way. However, do not answer questions—even if the school authorities say it is in your best interest to do so, or even if the police say you will not be allowed to leave until you have answered their questions.

There may be occasions when nothing bad would come of answering a few questions on the spot to clear up a simple misunderstanding, but it is hard to tell in advance what these situations are. You should keep in mind, however, that it is the job of the police to investigate crimes. If you have any reason to believe that you are suspected of committing a crime, do not explain, do not lie, do not confess. Don't talk, except to ask to call your parents or a lawyer.

The same rules apply to questioning by school officials, since what you say to a school official can be used against you in a criminal prosecution or in a suspension/expulsion hearing. For example, a California court upheld the conviction of a student on the basis of testimony by his high-school principal that the student had confessed in response to the principal's questioning to having purchased marijuana in school. The court held that the principal, not being a police officer, was not required to warn the student of his right to remain silent before questioning him, and thus the confession was admissible evidence. Remember: *Your silence can never be used against you.*

Can school officials search students in school?

Yes, under certain circumstances. The Fourth Amendment to the Constitution provides that "the right of the people to be secure in their persons, houses, papers and effects against unreasonable searches and seizures shall not be violated." In *New Jersey v. T.L.O.*,[1] the Supreme Court ruled that students in school have Fourth Amendment protections against unreasonable searches of their persons and property. The Court found that school authorities act as public officials, not private citizens, when they search students and such searches are, therefore, limited by the Fourth Amendment. A majority of the

115

justices, however, refused to apply to searches of students the usual Fourth Amendment requirements that before searching a citizen a government official must have a warrant signed by a judge or the express consent of the person searched. The Court said that requiring school officials to get a warrant based on "probable cause" to believe that a student had committed a crime would "unduly interfere with the maintenance of the swift and informal disciplinary procedures needed in schools." It therefore ruled that school officials can search a student:

> *when there are reasonable grounds for suspecting that the search will turn up evidence that the student has violated or is violating either the law or the rules of the school. Such a search will be permissible in its scope when the measures adopted are reasonably related to the objectives of the search and not excessively intrusive in light of the age and sex of the student and the nature of the infraction.*

This means that to be reasonable under *T.L.O.*, a school search must pass two tests. First, the school official must have good reason to think evidence of wrongdoing will be found. Second, the search must not be more extensive than necessary to find the specific thing the school official expects to find. For example, if a teacher is looking for a stolen CD and cassette player, he or she may be able to look in your locker, but not in your pockets.

The Supreme Court's *T.L.O.* decision sets out the student's minimum rights against unreasonable school searches. But states are free to set stricter standards than "reasonable suspicion" under their state laws and constitutions, and school districts can further restrict them. At least one state requires full probable cause for personal searches of students. For the most part, however, state courts have adopted the *T.L.O.* "reasonable suspicion" or "reasonable grounds" standards for school searches. These courts have listed a number of factors to be considered in determining whether there is sufficient cause to search a student. These include the student's age, history, and school record, as well as the prevalence and seriousness of the problem and the presence of an emergency—for example, a report of a weapon—requiring a search without delay or further investigation. Schools should also consider the strength and reliability of the evidence used to justify the search and the particular school official's prior experience with the student.

In several cases, state courts have found that school officials lacked sufficient cause for a student search. The California Supreme Court found unlawful a school principal's search of a student whom he suspected of being tardy or truant and who was carrying a bag with an "odd-looking bulge." When the principal attempted to see the bag, the student held it behind his back and told him he needed a warrant. The court found that these facts did not add up to a "reasonable suspicion" that the student was engaged in unlawful activity.

Similarly, the highest court in New York found no reasonable grounds for a drug search after a student had been seen twice within one hour entering a rest room with a fellow student and leaving within five to ten seconds. According to the court, these trips "could be explained by all sorts of innocent activities." In general, the court emphasized that "although the necessities for a public school search may be greater than for one outside the school, the psychological damage that would be risked on sensitive children by random search insufficiently justified by the necessities is not tolerable."

In Florida, a court found that an assistant principal did not have reasonable suspicion sufficient to justify searching a student when his female friend fainted at school, reportedly because she had taken drugs. On the other hand, a New York court found that a school security guard had acted reasonably when he felt the outside of a student's back bag and searched it upon hearing "a metallic thud" when the student put the bag on the floor.

Can school officials search a whole group of students to find out which one of them has done something wrong?

In the *T.L.O.* case, the Supreme Court did not have to deal with the question whether students may be subjected to mass searches, because the teacher's accusation pointed to only one student. A number of federal and state courts have ruled, however, that there must be reasonable suspicion directed at a specific student before a school official can search the student. For instance, in two Texas cases, federal courts ruled that a sniff search around students' bodies by police dogs trained to detect drugs was unconstitutional because there was no "individualized suspicion"—that is, suspicion of a particular student. Similarly, a state court in Washington ruled that school officials did not have reasonable suspicion when they made students agree to a search of their luggage as a condition for participating in a band concert without a particularized suspicion that prohibited items would be found on each student searched. In the same vein, a federal court in New York ruled that it was unreasonable to strip-search an entire fifth-grade class in order to identify the student who had stolen three dollars. Similarly, routine searches of every student referred to a dean for breaking a school rule, or random searches on Halloween to deter pranks, violate the rule that individualized reasonable suspicion is required as a basis for a student search.

Can students be subjected to strip searches?

In a strip search, the person being searched is required to

remove all or most of her or his clothes. Often such searches include a search of body cavities where objects can be secreted. Although courts have not banned strip searches outright, two important rules limit their use. First, the Supreme Court in *T.L.O.* prohibited searches that are "excessively intrusive." If a teacher is looking for a gun or large knife, a pat-down would be enough to determine whether the student had the weapon. On the other hand, a search for a small bag of missing candy might require a more intrusive search, but one that could not be justified in light of the relative unimportance of the infraction.

A number of courts have ruled that the more intrusive the search, the higher the degree of suspicion required. A federal court in New York, for instance, found that the teacher had reasonable suspicion to search a student's handbag for stolen money but should not have strip-searched the student without full probable cause. Along the same lines, a federal court in Indiana ruled that a strip search including a body cavity search of students based on a sniffer dog's alert was illegal: "The conduct of the school official's authority to conduct reasonable searches could not justify a degrading search of a student's body cavities."

In some communities, outrage over particular search incidents has resulted in school boards' passing detailed policies to protect student rights. In Louisville, Kentucky, for instance, such detailed search procedures were promulgated following an episode where an entire third-grade class was strip-searched because four dollars collected in a raffle were missing. The new rules require reasonable individualized suspicion and limit searches to accessories and outer garments. In cases where school officials believe that students possess evidence that could result in criminal charges or that a search may require "disrobing to the skin," the search must be conducted by law-enforcement officers.

After a similar incident, the Columbia, South Carolina, school district adopted a full probable-cause standard for strip searches of students. There, searches must be authorized and supervised by the principal, and students cannot be asked to expose underwear or private parts of the body.

Can school officials search students' desks and lockers?

Probably. State courts, statutes, and local practices vary widely on the question of when students' lockers and desks can be searched. But one thing is certain: School officials have fewer restrictions on searching lockers and desks than on searching persons, and in many places they are much freer. Therefore, good advice is: Do not put anything in your locker or desk that you would not want the police or school officials to see.

In one New York case, a vice-principal conducted a locker search at the direction of a police officer who suspected the student possessed drugs; the court upheld the search on the ground that the student had no reasonable expectation of privacy since he knew the principal had a master key to all the locks. Other courts have said schools can conduct locker searches triggered by drug-detecting dogs, because the school exercises control over the lockers.

In contrast, the California Supreme Court makes no distinction between personal searches and searches of lockers; in both situations it requires reasonable and individualized suspicion. Like California, New Jersey insists there be definite grounds for suspicion in order to search a locker. The New Jersey Supreme Court ruled that it was unlawful to search a locker in a case where a police officer had received an anonymous call from someone claiming to be the parent of another student and naming a certain student as a drug dealer. The officer passed this information on to the school and an assistant principal searched the student's locker. The court found that the information did not amount to reasonable suspicion, which was required for a locker search if, as here, the student was justified in believing that the master key to the locker would be used only at his request or convenience. If the school had a publicized policy of regularly inspecting student lockers, the suspected student might not have had the same expectation of privacy.

A number of states have statutes insisting upon reasonable suspicion before lockers can be searched, but do not require search warrants. Louisiana law, for instance, states that any teacher, principal, or administrator can search any "building, desk, locker, area or grounds" for contraband "when he has articulable facts which lead him to a reasonable belief that the items sought will be found."

In some states schools must notify students that their lockers are subject to search. One state limits such searches to items illegal under state law and requires that a third party be present when a locker is searched.

Many local school districts also have written policies on locker searches which vary in the protection of privacy. One school district permits locker searches but states "there must be reason to believe that the student is using his/her locker, desk or other property in such a way as to endanger his/her own health or safety or the health, safety and rights of other persons." In contrast, another school-district policy states that "desks and lockers are public property and school authorities may conduct an inspection for any reason related to school administration." Whether or not you have a reasonable expectation of privacy in your locker or desk may depend on the stated policy of your particular school.

Can schools require students to submit to blood and urine tests for drugs?

Requiring a person to give a blood or urine sample so that it can be tested for the presence of illegal drugs is considered a search under the Fourth Amendment. Recently, many school districts have imposed such tests on students in an attempt to combat drug and alcohol use.

In *Veronia School District 47J v. Acton,*[2] a student challenged the policy of the school district of randomly testing the urine of all student athletes for drugs. First, he argued that urinating is something that people do in private behind closed doors and that it therefore is an invasion of privacy to have a school official watch while you urinate. Second, he argued that it was an invasion of privacy to have school officials learn the information that would be disclosed by the test. For example, the test reveals not only the presence of illegal drugs, but also of prescription medication, which the student might not want school officials to know about.

The Supreme Court rejected the student's arguments and held that the school policy was valid. The Court found that drug use among students in the school district had become a major problem. It also found that students necessarily gave up a good deal of their right to privacy when they joined athletic teams. For example, they regularly undressed and showered together. As for the problem of the information revealed by the test, the Court said that it certainly would be possible for school officials to avoid gaining unnecessary knowledge by having the urine samples sent directly to a lab for testing and requesting the lab to reveal only the information concerning the presence of illegal drugs. The Court concluded that the benefits of the testing outweighed the minor invasion of privacy.

But the Supreme Court in *Acton* made it very clear indeed that its decision did not mean that random urine testing of an entire student body would be permissible; it simply did not decide that issue. The Court's reasoning concerning privacy does not seem to apply to such wide-scale testing, however, since students in general do not voluntarily give up their privacy rights when they are compelled to go to school the way student athletes do by voluntarily joining teams.

Can evidence illegally obtained be used to prosecute or discipline a student?

When the police search someone illegally, whatever evidence they discover cannot be used against the person at trial. This is called the "exclusionary rule" because the evidence is excluded from trial.

A number of state courts have ruled that just as in the case of searches by police, evidence obtained by means of an unlawful search by a school official may not be used against a student. Most of these cases, however, were ones in which criminal prosecutions or delinquency proceedings had been brought as the result of a school search. It is less clear whether the exclusionary rule applies in a school disciplinary hearing. Some courts have held that schools may not use evidence obtained in an unconstitutional search as grounds to punish students, whereas other courts have reached the opposite conclusion. For example, New York's highest court has held that a school superintendent had acted legally when he suspended a student who was caught carrying a loaded gun to school, even though a judge had held the search illegal.

What rules govern in-school searches by police?

Unlike school officials, police must obey all of the requirements of the Fourth Amendment in schools as well as on the street. If the security guards in your school have the power to make an arrest, they are viewed as police rather than as school officials for purposes of determining when they may conduct a search. However, even police may make a warrantless search in an emergency when "exigent circumstances"—a real emergency such as someone shouting "He's got a gun!"—make it likely that someone will be hurt or evidence will be destroyed if they wait for a warrant. Police can also make a warrantless search of a person and areas within her or his immediate reach at the time of an arrest. Police can stop and frisk a person without full probable cause or a warrant if the police officer has a reasonable basis to believe that there is criminal activity under way and that the suspect is armed. A lawful frisk must be limited to a pat-down of outer clothing strictly for the purpose of discovering weapons.

How can you protect yourself against an unlawful search?

In case of a search of your person or locker, desk, etc., the best you can do is to follow these rules:

1. Never carry on you or keep in school anything that you would not want the police or school officials to know about for any reason.

2. Never consent to any search. Say in a loud, clear voice, so that witnesses can hear, that you do not consent. But do not resist if a policeman or school official goes ahead with the search. If you do not consent to the search, there is a possibility that anything found on you will not be able to be used against you in court or in disciplinary proceedings. If you consent, it can and may be used.

10

GRADES AND DIPLOMAS

**Can a student challenge academic decisions of
school officials in court?**

Almost never. As a general rule, courts refuse to intervene in
cases in which students wish to challenge the academic decisions of administrators. Thus, if you believe you should have
received an A rather than a B on a test or essay, do not expect
a court to help you out. The exception to this rule is where a
student's claim is that the school's decision to lower a grade or
deny a diploma was not based on an evaluation of academic
performance, but was for some other, non-academic reason
such as racial bias.

**Can a student be denied a diploma as punishment
for misconduct?**

Probably not. But schools occasionally do deny students a diploma as punishment for misconduct, despite the fact that they
have fulfilled all the academic requirements for graduation.

125

Although few legal precedents exist in this area, a 1971 decision of the chancellor of the New York City schools, binding on all high schools in that city, is significant. The ruling arose in the following situation. The New York high school diploma mentioned "citizenship" as well as academic achievement, and a principal temporarily withheld the diploma of a student who, he felt, was not a "good citizen," even though the student had completed all his academic work for graduation. The chancellor disagreed. In holding that the diploma must be issued, he wrote:

> *Students who violate rules of conduct are subject to disciplinary measures, but the manipulation of a diploma is not a proper or legitimate disciplinary tool in view of the inherent difficulty of defining "citizenship" and the clear danger and impropriety of labelling students as "good" or "bad" citizens. The school system should award the diploma on the basis of carefully defined educational criteria, and not deny or delay the diploma on other than educational grounds or as a means of discipline. In brief, the school is empowered to grant diplomas, not citizenship.*

Can students be denied diplomas for failing statewide competency exams?

Maybe. Several cases have been brought to challenge the denial of diplomas to students who have met all of their schools' academic requirements but have failed statewide, standardized competency tests. The courts have come to different conclusions, but the general rule appears to be that the requirement that students pass such tests in order to graduate is legal, as long as material covered by the test has been covered in school. Courts agree that it is unfair to test students on subjects they have never been taught.

Can a student be denied a diploma for failing gym?

The law is unclear in most states. The New York State Commissioner of Education ruled in 1971 that "boards of education may not refuse graduation or promotion because of failure in physical education." Students therefore must be granted diplomas even if they are not able to perform certain required exercises.

Failing to participate in a required gym class may be treated differently from inability to perform well in gym. Although a California court ordered a school to reverse its refusal to graduate a student who had been given a failing grade in physical education for refusing to run laps around the gymnasium as punishment for being on the losing side of a volleyball game, students run a clear risk in not attending if gym is a required subject. If an attempt is made to keep you from graduating because you cut gym, you have several possible arguments. If you were not given advance notice of the consequences of cutting gym, then your due-process rights were violated. If other students are exempted from gym or their absence is simply overlooked, then the rule is not being applied consistently, and denying you a diploma would be unfair.

11

SCHOOL RECORDS

Every school makes a record of each student's academic and personal progress from the time she or he enters kindergarten until she or he graduates, and often it keeps this cumulative record for many years afterward. The record may include, as was noted in one New York case, "progress reports, subject grades, intelligence quotients, tests, achievement scores, medical records, psychological and psychiatric reports, selective guidance notes and the evaluations of students by educators." In short, your school keeps a great deal of personal information about you permanently on file.

The National Education Association's *Code of Student Rights and Responsibilities* states: "Records are kept to assist the school in offering appropriate educational experiences to the student. The interest of the student must supersede all other purposes to which records might be put."

In practice, the reverse is often the case. School officials frequently use a student's record against him or her as a threat

("If you do that again, it will go in your record and end up in your college recommendations") or as the basis for a suspension or other serious disciplinary action. Often the information contained in school records is little more than an expression of personal opinion of the student by teachers and other school personnel. Such remarks as "[student] spoke strangely to girls in class"; "never gives anyone benefit of doubt"; "Black militant"; "disrespectful while class was saluting flag"; and "is unkind to old people" have appeared in the permanent records of students in the New York City schools.

At least one court has recognized that student records are not supposed to be gossip sheets, and it ordered a high-school principal to expunge from a student's record a notation that he had criticized the school and the principal on a radio program. New Hampshire specifically bars schools from keeping records "which reflect the political activities or beliefs of students." It is also one of the few states that require cumulative records to be destroyed when they are no longer current.

Do students have the right to see their own records?

Yes. The biggest problems that arise in connection with school records concern who has access to them. On the one hand, many schools maintain that records are so confidential that students and their parents cannot see them; on the other, schools sometimes allow anyone else who claims to have a legitimate interest—such as a police officer, social worker, or potential employer—to see these same confidential records. The right to have petty personal comments expunged from your record does not mean much if you cannot find out they are there; and even without gossip, your record contains personal information that you probably would not want many people to see. Fortunately, not only have courts recognized the

129

dangers of school record-keeping, but federal legislation gives students the right to see to their own records while limiting the public's right to see it.

In 1974, Congress passed an amendment to the Family Educational Rights and Privacy Act. Called the Buckley Amendment,[1] it guarantees the parents of students (and students themselves who are over eighteen or attending a postsecondary school) the right to examine their children's student records, provided the school receives some sort of federal funding. The law applies to virtually every public institution and many private ones. State and local laws in many areas have applied the Buckley Amendment to all schools. The law assumes that both parents have the right to access, unless a court order or a binding legal agreement such as a custody agreement provides otherwise.

Under the Buckley Amendment, a student under eighteen can see her or his records if the school decides on its own to give the student access, or if the parent tells the school in writing to do so. There are a few restrictions on access that apply to students but not to parents. For example, parents, but not students, are given access to psychiatric and other noneducational treatment records in the sole possession of those providing treatment. But students who are at least eighteen can designate a physician or certain other professionals whom the school must permit to inspect these records. Students may see confidential letters of recommendation unless they have waived the right to see them. Even then, they may see them if they are being used other than for the purpose for which the waiver was given.

The Buckley Amendment provides that schools must respond to a request to view records "within a reasonable period of time." This period can never exceed 45 days, but many states and cities specify shorter periods and impose additional restrictions. In Massachusetts, for instance, schools must honor requests within two consecutive weekdays, may charge a reasonable fee for the cost of copies made of documents, and may insist that school officials be present during an inspection of the original records. Some states—for example, Oregon—require schools to provide the services of a person qualified to interpret or explain behavioral records if they are being released.

In New York City and Massachusetts, the school is required to notify parents every year of their right to see their child's records.

Do students and parents have a right to see special-education records?

Yes. Parents have the right to "inspect and review" any education records relating to the student if the records are collected, maintained, or used pursuant to the Buckley Amendment. Even medical or psychological records, under the Buckley Amendment, should be available to parents if they are part of the student's evaluation or included in the student's school files. This is especially true if the records concern diagnosis, since even the Buckley Amendment limits access to records concerning "treatment."

The best protection against the accumulation of irrelevant or inaccurate information in a student's file is for parents to regularly inspect their children's records. Part of the reason that school officials are able to keep records that are frequently based on little more than hearsay and rumor is their assumption that no parent or student will ever ask to see the records. If more parents demanded to see records, school officials might be more careful in checking their facts.

What can a student do about improper or inaccurate entries in her or his school records?

Upon checking your records, if you find that they contain material that you believe is inaccurate or unfair, you have a right under the Buckley Amendment, to meet informally with school officials to ask them to change the records. If they refuse, you have a right to a formal hearing, to be held within a reasonable time before an impartial hearing officer, at which you must have a full opportunity to present your side of the story. The decision, in writing, must also be rendered within a reasonable time.

If the decision is not to amend the record, the parent or eligible student may still place a statement into the records explaining why the entry is unfair or inaccurate. This explanation must be included anytime the contested portion of a record is released to anyone.

In some school districts, students are permitted to contest the accuracy of any entry in their records and, if still not satisfied, to add their own version of the incident, before or instead of a formal hearing. Some districts require parents to be notified promptly whenever a derogatory remark is placed in their child's record and have the right to appeal to have it expunged before going to a formal hearing.

Even if an entry is proper, it may not be appropriate to keep it on a student's record forever. Many school districts have policies about periodically reviewing and destroying outdated or irrelevant information in students' temporary or guidance records. In New York City public high schools, this review is supposed to take place twice a year. In Massachusetts, parents are supposed to be notified before temporary records are destroyed, in case they want to see them first. Again, it is important to inspect records at least once a year to make sure they do not contain more than they should.

Do students have the right to have school records kept confidential from outsiders?

Yes. The Buckley Amendment also provides that educational institutions must obtain the written consent of a student's parents before it may release personally identifiable data to any-one other than a specified list of persons, such as school offi-cials or teachers within the school who have a "legitimate educational interest" in the student's records. Records can also be sent to a school to which the student is transferring, but only after the parent has a chance to request a copy and chal-lenge anything improper. Schools may turn over records in compliance with a lawful court order or subpoena only if they make a reasonable effort to notify the parent before they com-ply. They may turn over student records in an emergency only if the information disclosed is strictly necessary to protect the health or safety of the student or others. "Directory informa-tion" such as name, address, telephone number, or academic major can be released to the general public only if the school notifies parents each year as to what information will be released. The parent may request that the school not include the student on the list. A log must be kept as part of the stu-dent's records, indicating which third parties have requested or obtained information and why they were given access. Some states have additional protections.

Some schools ask parents at the beginning of a school year, or at the time when their children first enter school, to sign a form which, among other things, gives the school the authority to release, at its own discretion, information from student records to inquiring outsiders. This kind of blanket authoriza-tion leads to many abuses. Parents may be happy to release certain information to a social worker, but unwilling to release the same information to the police department. They may also change their minds about the release of their child's school record when certain new information is added. By requesting parents to sign a blanket authorization for release of informa-tion, the school is asking them to sign away rights concerning their child. Instead, parents should ask that their permission be obtained each time the school wishes to release information.

Finally, if a parent or a student over eighteen tells the school in writing to release specified records to someone else such as a lawyer, relative, counselor, or friend, the school must comply.

When do students, rather than their parents, have the right of control over school records?

Under the Buckley Amendment, at the age of eighteen or whenever a student starts to attend a postsecondary school, students rather than their parents have access to and control over the release of their school records. Different laws exist in some states. Delaware, for example, permits students from the age of fourteen to control the release of their own records. In Massachusetts, once a student reaches age fourteen or enters ninth grade, the student has the same rights as her or his parents regarding school records. In New York City, high-school students can see their permanent school records (e.g., grades, attendance, test scores) without parental permission, but they need parental permission to view their guidance records.

12

PRIVATE SCHOOLS

The discussion of student rights in this book is mainly applicable to public school students. That is not to say, however, that private and parochial (religious) school students have no rights.

Can private schools discriminate on the basis of race?

No. The Supreme Court has ruled that private, non-religious schools are prohibited from discriminating on the basis of race by the Civil Rights Act of 1866, commonly referred to as Section 1981. The act was passed by Congress to eradicate all vestiges of slavery after the Thirteenth Amendment abolished slavery. The Supreme Court has not decided whether parochial schools are prohibited from practicing racial discrimination (for example, expulsions for interracial dating) that is based on religious doctrine, although some courts have said that such schools may be required to pay taxes, which other schools do not have to do, if they discriminate. Some lower federal courts have held that it is illegal for parochial schools to exclude black students from admission and to expel white students for interracial dating. They have concluded that the religious schools acted from political or social beliefs, not religious principles, so that the free exercise of religion clause of the First Amendment was not violated.

Even religious grounds do not justify discrimination, according to one panel of judges that heard a racial exclusion case in 1978. While they saw a school's exclusionary policies as based on religious belief, they said the need to eradicate the badges of slavery outweighed the right to free exercise of religion.

Can private schools discriminate on the basis of national origin, sex, or disability?

The federal circuit courts are divided on whether discrimination on the basis of national origin is also prohibited by Section 1981. However, under Title VI of the Civil Rights Act of 1964, discrimination on the basis of race, color, or national origin is prohibited in any school program or activity that receives money from the federal government.

While Section 1981 does not apply to discrimination on the basis of gender or disability, such discrimination is also prohibited for any program or activity receiving federal funds. Section 504 of the Rehabilitation Act of 1973 forbids exclusion, discrimination, or denial of benefits on the basis of disability, while Title IX of the Education Amendments of 1972 contains the same prohibitions on discrimination based on gender. The Supreme Court has interpreted these statutes to cover only the specific activity or program that receives federal funding, not the school as a whole.

Students with disabilities who are placed in private schools by a public agency at public expense are guaranteed the same rights as disabled students in public schools. Disabled children who attend private schools but were not placed there by public agencies are still entitled to publicly funded special-education services if they need them.

Do private school students have due-process rights?

Private and parochial school students may have due-process rights, but not necessarily for the same reasons or to the same extent as public school students. The Fourteenth Amendment applies to "state action," that is, action by an official or an agency of state or local government. Courts look for state action in a private school on a case-by-case basis. They ask whether the school as a whole is under the control of or acting on behalf of the government, and they inquire whether a government agency shares responsibility for the specific act or activity that is being challenged, through, for example, government regulation or financial aid. The courts generally conclude there is no state action.

A private school student may, however, have a contractual right to due process. School catalogs and handbooks are considered by courts to be part of the contract between the buyer of educational services (the student) and the seller (the school). If the literature says that a hearing will be held before a student is expelled, then the student has a contractual right to such a hearing. In one case where a university specifically provided for a hearing before expulsion of a student, a court said it would review the procedures to make sure they met the "reasonable expectations" of a student reading the relevant university rules and would examine the hearing to make sure it had been conducted fairly. But the same court said that it would not question the school's decision to expel or suspend a student if there was no stated policy providing for a hearing. In another case, the court held that students had no right to notice or a hearing before an expulsion because, according to the catalog, the school reserved the right to expel without mentioning a hearing.

A different line of cases says that private institutions must have fair procedures not because of any contractual agreement, but because students have interests in their degrees and in their reputations that the courts should protect. These cases balance student interests against the importance of the private school's integrity and independence. In one such case, where a student was suspended for one year for allegedly violating Princeton University's honor code, the court concluded, "Princeton must have established procedures for safeguarding [the student's] interest, and, if it strays from its own rules, Princeton must have good and sufficient reasons for doing so." In another case, the court said that Princeton could not have someone arrested for criminal trespass for selling political materials on its campus because the university did not have a reasonable regulatory scheme designed to protect both its legitimate interests as an institution of higher education and the individual exercise of freedom of expression. In a third case, a New York court ruled that "a private university cannot expel, bar and fine a student without following fair and reasonable procedures. It cannot be arbitrary. It must abide by constitutional principles of fair conduct implicit in our society."

Can private schools expel students for bad grades?

Private schools probably have more discretion to expel a student for poor academic performance than for disciplinary reasons. Courts do not want to second-guess schools on academic standards and will overturn such expulsions only if the school has acted in an arbitrary and capricious fashion. In one case, a court did order a school to readmit a student because an appeals committee had allowed other students who had failed the same number of courses to repeat the year's work. The court found that the school's failure to apply its procedures and standards equally to all students was unfair and an abuse of discretion. But in a different sort of case, a student leader with an otherwise blameless record was accused of plagiarism after failing to attribute the source of a quote on a term paper. Here the court upheld the university's decision to withhold the student's bachelor's degree for a year, saying that it would not "engraft its own views" on a private school's student disciplinary process, so long as that process met the "standard of good faith and fair-dealing."

Do private school students have rights regarding non-public school records?

The Family Education Rights and Privacy Act (the Buckley Amendment), which protects the privacy of student records and requires schools to show records on request to parents or to adult students, applies to only those non-public schools that receive federal funds. Few private schools below the college level receive federal funds. Some states and cities, however, have applied the Buckley Amendment to all schools through statute or regulation. Others have open-record laws that apply to any school that receives state funds.

Sometimes schools try to withhold student transcripts because of unpaid tuition. A Texas attorney general said that one such school could lose its accreditation if it did not allow parents to "inspect and review" student records, because the school participated in a federal school-lunch program and was therefore covered by the Buckley Amendment. A California attorney general ruled that under state law, both public and private schools are obligated to transfer records upon the request of the school to which a student has transferred, because withholding records might mean the student could not attend school, as required by state law. Similarly, a New York court ordered a private school to honor a parent's request that a transcript be sent to the student's new school, even though tuition was owed.

NOTES

Decisions of the federal courts are contained in multivolume sets of books known as the Federal Supplement (abbreviated "F.Supp.") for the district courts, the Federal Reporter (abbreviated "F.," "F.2d.," or "F.3d") for the courts of appeals, and United States Reports (abbreviated "U.S.") or Supreme Court Reports (abbreviated "S.Ct.") for the Supreme Court. The names of the parties involved in the case come first, next the volume number, next the name of the reporter, next the page on which the case begins, next the name of the court, and finally the date of the decision. For example, 376 F.Supp. 750 (M.D.Fla. 1974) means that the case appears in volume 376 of the Federal Supplement on page 750 and was decided by the district court for the middle district of Florida in 1974. The librarian at a law school or a library that has law books can help you locate any of the decisions that are cited in this book. The decisions are also available online through Westlaw and Lexis, and through the World Wide Web.

CHAPTER 3

1. *Brown v. Board of Education,* 347 U.S. 483 (1954).

2. *Plyler v. Doe,* 457 U.S. 202 (1982).

3. Education of Individuals with Disabilities Act, 20 U.S.C. § 1400 *et seq.* See also Americans with Disabilities Act, 42 U.S.C. § 12101 *et seq.*

CHAPTER 4

1. *Tinker v. Des Moines Indep. Community School Dist.,* 393 U.S. 503 (1969).

2. *Bethel School Dist. No. 403 v. Fraser,* 478 U.S. 675 (1969).

3. *Hazelwood School Dist. v. Kuhlmeier,* 484 U.S. 260 (1987).

4. *Board of Educ., Island Trees Union Free School Dist. No. 26 v. Pico,* 457 U.S. 853 (1969).

5. *West Virginia State Board of Educ. v. Barnette,* 319 U.S. 624 (1943).

CHAPTER 5

1. *Engel v. Vitale,* 370 U.S. 421 (1962).

2. *Wallace v. Jaffree,* 472 U.S. 38 (1985).

3. *Lee v. Weisman,* 505 U.S. 577 (1972).

4. *Zorach v. Clauson,* 343 U.S. 306 (1952).

5. *Stone v. Graham,* 449 U.S. 39 (1980).

6. 20 U.S.C. § 4071 *et seq.*

CHAPTER 7

1. *Goss v. Lopez,* 419 U.S. 565 (1975).

CHAPTER 8

1. *Ingraham v. Wright*, 430 U.S. 651 (1977).

CHAPTER 9

1. *New Jersey v. T.L.O.*, 469 U.S. 325 (1985).
2. *Veronia School Dist. 47J v. Acton*, 115 S.Ct. 2386 (1995).

CHAPTER 11

1. P.L. 93–380, 20 U.S.C. § 1232 (g).

RESOURCES

ORGANIZATIONS

American Civil Liberties Union
132 W. 43rd Street
New York, NY 10036
(212) 944-9800

The telephone number is the organization's automated service line. There is a touch-tone menu, and the public-relations department can be reached through it. The number for obtaining a free catalog of ACLU publications is 1-800-775-ACLU.

U.S. Department of Education
75 Park Place
New York, NY 10007
General Information: (212) 264-7005
(800) 424-1616
Civil Rights: (212) 637-6466

143

The main telephone number at the United States Department of Education is just a starting point. The switchboard can direct callers to divisions that handle particular areas of the law, such as bilingual education. The department's clearinghouse provides actual documents for researchers.

National Library of Education
(800) 424-1616

This organization provides information about literature on student rights.

Education Research Clearing House
(800) 538-3742

This number allows a person to connect to a database system of 900,000 documents published by sixteen clearinghouses with varying areas of expertise on subjects of concern to students. The operators who answer the telephones are very helpful.

National Coalition Against Censorship
275 7th Avenue
New York, NY 10001
(212) 807-6222

This office deals with issues of public-school students' First Amendment rights.

National Committee for Public Education and Religious Liberty
165 E. 56th Street
New York, NY 10022
(212) 750-6461

Clearinghouse for parents, teachers, and students. Provides information on pro bono attorneys; deals with separation of church and state issues and is affiliated with ACLU.

144

FOR FURTHER READING

The Rights of Women. American Civil Liberties Union Handbook by Susan Deller Ross and Ann Barcher. Carbondale, Illinois: Southern Illinois University Press, 1993.

The book contains a section on sex discrimination in education.

Choosing Equality: The Case for Democratic Schooling by A. Bastian, N. Fruchter, C. Greer, M. Gittell, and K. Haskins. Philadelphia, Pennsylvania: Temple University Press, 1989.

School Discipline and Student Rights: An Advocate's Manual by Paul Weckstein. Center for Law and Education; Cambridge, Mass., 1982.

This book is appropriate for use by adults who are advocating on behalf of students in school disciplinary hearings.

Special Education: A Manual for Advocates by Diana Pullin. Center for Law and Education: Cambridge, Mass., 1982.

This two-volume work provides, among other information, an overview of federal law governing education of the handicapped, including an appendix listing the relevant federal regulations and statutes; a description of persons who qualify as handicapped or in need of or subject to special education pursuant to federal law; and an examination of education programs and testing and placement of children. The book consists mainly of raw data that would be of interest to a professional audience, but the bibliography and appendices are extensive and non-professionals will find it useful.

Public School Law: Teachers' and Students' Rights by Martha M. McCarthy and Nelda H. Cambron. Boston: Allyn and Bacon, 1981. The second half of this book pertains to student rights. It covers topics such as school discipline, corporal punishment, dress codes, and First Amendment rights. The book

145

would probably be most useful to a reader with a little legal background, but it is accessible to others.

Search and Seizure in the Public Schools by Lawrence T. Rossow and Jacqueline Stefkovich. Topeka, Kan.: National Organization on Legal Problems of Education, 1995. An examination of recent cases addressing the search and seizure issues; includes a discussion of formal legal aspects of the topic. It is accessible to a high-school student as far as language is concerned, but it is probably more useful to one writing a research paper, not one trying to ascertain her or his individual rights. It is current, focused, and comprehensive.

Student's Legal Rights and Responsibilities by Michael W. Lamorte, Harold W. Gentry, and D. Parker Young. Cincinnati, Ohio: W.H. Anderson Co., 1971.

With its emphasis on student responsibilities, this book resembles an annotated school handbook. It reads very much like a generic book of school regulations, replete with explanations of why certain regulations might be implemented, and illustrated with certain cases. It is definitely geared to a young-adult audience. Its treatment of the subject is comprehensive.

Ability Grouping of Public School Students by Joseph E. Bryson and Charles P. Bently. Charlottesville, Va.: Michie Co., 1980.

This book is well written, but a legal background is helpful. It is suitable for use by adults who are involved with young people on issues of ability grouping of students. The organization of the book is good, the table of contents effective, and both help direct an inexperienced reader to her or his topic easily.

The Rights of Religious Persons in Public Education by John W. Whitehead. Illinois: Cressway Books, 1994.

This book could be renamed *Everything You Wanted to Know About the Rights of Religious Persons in Public*

Schools, But Were Afraid to Ask. It is a handbook, plain and simple.

Standards Relating to Schools and Education by the Joint Commission on Juvenile Justice Standards. Cambridge, Mass.; Balliner Pub. Co., 1967.

This book provides basic guidelines for implementing school regulations. It is excellent background material, but difficult reading. Therefore it is most appropriate for use by adults who are working with students on developing school regulations.

INDEX

C

California:

corporal punishment statute, 108*n.*

expulsion in, 80, 95, 99

extracurricular activities, fees for, 11

out-of-school activities, limited authority over, 73

school records in, 139–40

search and seizure standards in, 117, 120

sex quotas in, 15

suspension in, 92

uniforms, wearing of, 67

Child abuse, 110

Children, laws pertaining solely to, 3

Choice of public school, 9–10

Citizenship, 17–18

Civil Rights Act of 1866 (Section 1981), 135, 136

Civil Rights Act of 1964, Title VI of, 136

Cleveland, Ohio, 113–14

Clothing:

advertising alcohol, 37

bearing messages, 36–37

dress codes, 37, 64–67

uniforms, 67

Clubs, 47–48, 63

Columbia, South Carolina, school district, 120

Competency exams, denial of diploma for failing, 126

Connecticut:

corporal punishment statute, 108*n.*

suspensions in, due process protections for, 90

Constitution, U.S., 1

Bill of Rights, 1–3

Fifth Amendment, 3, 96, 113

First Amendment:

freedom of assembly, 2, 49

freedom of expression, 2, 26

power of, 76
racial discrimination in, 104–106
state law and, 79
see also Suspension
Extracurricular activities:
athletics, *see* Athletics
being forbidden to participate in, 82–84
fees for, 11–12
married students, participation by, 19–21
pregnant students, participation by, 19–21
students with children, participation by, 19–21

F

Family Educational Rights and Privacy Act, Buckley
    Amendment to, 130–34, 139
Federal courts, 4–5
Felonies, 80
Fingerprinting for identification, 113
First Amendment rights, *see* Constitution, U.S., First Amendment
Flag-saluting ceremonies, 55–56
Florida:
out-of-school activities, limited authority over, 73
search and seizure standards in, 117–118
suspension in, 80
Fourteenth Amendment, *see* Constitution, U.S., Fourteenth
    Amendment
Fourth Amendment, *see* Search and seizure, protection from
    unreasonable
Fraser, Matthew, 29–30
Freedom of expression:
when both sides of a controversy are banned, 40–41
buttons, armbands, or clothing bearing messages, 28–29, 36–37
"clear and present danger" of violence, 34
clubs and organizations, forming, 47–48
content of expression, 34–35

G

Eve Cary, a professor at Brooklyn Law School in New York, is a former staff attorney with the New York Civil Liberties Union. She is the general editor of the ACLU's series of rights books and is the coauthor of *The Rights of Students*, on which this book is based. She is also the coauthor of *New York Criminal Law, Appellate Advocacy: Principles and Practice,* and *Woman and the Law.*

Alan H. Levine, a constitutional lawyer, was formerly a staff attorney with the New York Civil Liberties Union and director of its Student Rights Project. He was Director of the Constitutional Law Clinic at Hofstra University School of Law, and has also taught constitutional law at Cardozo and New York University Schools of Law. He has written, lectured and litigated extensively in the area of student rights as well as in other areas of constitutional law. At present he is a Visiting Scholar at the Columbia University Center for the Study of Human Rights and the recipient of a grant from the John D. and Catherine T. MacArthur Foundation Program on International Peace and Cooperation to work on a project involving international human rights and indigenous peoples.

Janet R. Price is currently teaching at International High School at LaGuardia Community College, a public school for new immigrants. She is the former Executive Vice President of New Visions for Public Schools, a school reform group for which she continues to do research and policy analysis. She serves on the board of Advocates for Children of New York, Inc., an organization that provides advocacy for New York City public school students where she previously served as managing attorney. She has served as the chair of the Committee on Education of the Law of the Association of the Bar of the City of New York, as a Revson Fellow for the Future of the City of New York at Columbia University, and as a board member of the National Coalition of Advocates for Students. She is the author of numerous and articles on school reform issues.